MW01287155

PAT BUTTRAM
ROCKING-CHAIR HUMORIST

Also by Sandra Grabman

Spotlights & Shadows: The Albert Salmi Story

Plain Beautiful: The Life of Peggy Ann Garner

No Retakes!
  (with Wright King)

Lloyd Nolan: An Actor's Life With Meaning
  (with Joel Blumberg)

PAT BUTTRAM
ROCKING-CHAIR HUMORIST

by Sandra Grabman

BearManor Media
2010

Pat Buttram: The Rocking-Chair Humorist

© 2010 Sandra Grabman

All rights reserved.

For information, address:

BearManor Media
P. O. Box 1129
Duncan, OK 73534

bearmanormedia.com

Title page sketch courtesy of Jack Lane

Cover design by John Teehan

Typesetting and layout by John Teehan

Published in the USA by BearManor Media

ISBN—1-59393-426-2

Acknowledgements

A **great big "Thank you!"** goes to members of Pat's warm and gracious family for their help and enthusiasm for this project. Included under this category, listed alphabetically, are his brother, Rev. Gus Buttram, and Gus' wife Rebecca, nephew John Buttram, nephew Rev. Mac Buttram, niece Harriet Delius and her husband Dan, niece and family historian Zella Fuller, daughter Kerry Galgano, daughter Gayle Gangl, sister Hallie Reed, and niece Mary Young.

Appreciated, too, are the memories and photos shared with me by his many friends, co-stars, stuntmen, and others: Michael Alley, Mrs. Gene Autry, Gene Autry Entertainment, Don Barnett, Dale Berry, Earl Blair, Jeanne De Vivier Brown, Karla Buhlman, Caruth Byrd, Harry Carey, Jr., Jim Ciardi, Sue Clark Chadwick, "Courage-Bagge," Robert Fuller, Holly George-Warren, Larry Given, Bill Hale, Mark Holton, Irynne Isip, Marty Lalperin, Maxine Hansen, Whitey Hughes, Ron Kamrowski, Hal Kanter, Wright King, Tom Lester, George Lindsey, William Malin, Randal Malone, Donna Martell, Bob Morgan, Jim Roberts, Jim Rorie, Bob Simons, Jon Smith, Chuck Southcott, Beverly Taliaferro, Johnny Western, and Jimmie Willhelm.

Also, these very kind people helped me with my research: Anna Alexander, Fred Beeman, Jason Bracht, Marcia Braunstein, Karla Buhlman, Michael Creech, Jeff Davis, Celia Foster, Clifford Gretano, Lorri Lee Lesher, Pamela Martin, Joe Postove, Michael Schramm, and Charles Stumpf.

Books:

The Alfred Hitchcock Presents Companion, by Martin Grams. Jr. and Patrick Wikstrom.

Singing in the Saddle: The History of the Singing Cowboy, by Douglas B. Green.

Television Westerns Episode Guide, All United States Series, 1949-1996, by Harris M. Lentz III.

Those Great Cowboy Sidekicks, by David Rothel.

Periodicals:

The Anniston Star, The Beverly Hills Citizen, The Birmingham News, The Birmingham Post-Herald, Chicago Daily News, (L.A.) Daily News, Hollywood Citizen-News, The Hollywood Reporter, Huntsville News, The L.A. Times, Mansfield Journal (Ohio), *Mountain Democrat, Movieland Magazine, Music City News, The National Enquirer, Parade Magazine, The Prairie Farmer, Radio Varieties, Rural Radio, Sheboyken Press, Stand By, Syracuse Herald-American, The Tampa Tribune, Times Daily, TV Guide, TV Life, TV-Radio Annual, TV-Radio Life, TV Radio Mirror, WLS Family Albums.*

Other Publications:

Academy Players Directory #41 and *The Gene Autry Show Souvenir Program* by Kathleen Lamb.

Organizations:

The Fairbanks Center for Motion Picture Study, The Gene Autry Museum, The Golden Boot Awards organization, The Masquers Club, The Motion Picture & Television Fund, and WLS radio.

Introduction

Pat **Buttram** has been the source of laughter and joy to me since I was a child in the 1950s. The tension caused by Gene Autry's pursuit of the bad guys on his television program was broken by his yodel-y-voiced sidekick, Pat, who had the wonderful ability of turning our frowns into smiles.

During my teen years, Pat reappeared on TV, this time as a regular on the delightful comedy *Green Acres*. Again, we'd begin laughing when he made his entrance each week because we knew his character, Mr. Haney, would do his level best to con Mr. Douglas out of a few bucks. He was usually successful, too.

"What was Pat Buttram really like?" I wondered. Was he the typical comedian who was the embodiment of merriment on stage, but glum when the cameras weren't rolling? Were all his hilarious lines written for him, or did he "think funny?"

Wanting to get to the bottom of this, I went to his family, friends, and cronies in showbiz and asked them to share their memories with me. What they taught me about Pat Buttram reaffirmed my conviction that I have excellent taste in men. Pat was even funnier offstage. He wrote not only much of his own material, but that of some of his friends, as well. Would you believe President Reagan? Yep, Pat gifted him with some nifty one-liners that were delivered with a merry sparkle in our President's eyes.

As Robert Benchley told Pat, he was not a comedian; rather, he was a humorist. There is a distinct difference, and Benchley recognized Buttram's talent for what it was.

Pat was a very good man who loved to make people happy. He had a soft heart for charities, as well, and lent his talents to their success.

In looking back at his life, I get the feeling that it was meant to be. Pat was born to bring us laughter and happiness. Things fell so neatly into place in his career that a Divine Hand just had to be involved.

My purpose in writing this book was not only to tell you the life story of this brilliant man, but also to bring a smile to your face. Throughout the book, I have included many of Pat's jokes for your enjoyment. If they make you laugh, my goal will be achieved.

Chapter One

The date was June 19, 1915. The place was Addison, Alabama, population two hundred. On the little back porch of the rural parsonage, four-year-old Hallie Buttram was frightened. Something scary seemed to be going on inside the house, and she and her two-year-old brother Gus had been sent outside. Their older siblings—Peggy, Mamie, Johnny, and Corry—were elsewhere. Now, nine decades later, the events of that night make much more sense to Hallie. Their baby brother, Maxwell Emmett Buttram, was being born. Someday, the world would know him as Pat, but that nickname would come later in his childhood. Both of little Maxwell's given names had been surnames of his ancestors.

The house in which big brother Gus was born in 1913 had originally been a saloon, but was converted into a Methodist parsonage, and the house in which Maxwell was born had originally been a church before its conversion. Thus, it became a family joke that Gus, who would someday become a minister, was born in a saloon while Maxwell, who would someday perform in establishments that served alcohol, was the one born in a church.

Their father, Wilson McDaniel "Mack" Buttram, had something in common with his new son right away: Each was the seventh child in his family. Mack had first met his wife, Mary Emmett Maxwell, when her mother was his Sunday School teacher at Mount Hope. They were married in 1901 at Maxwell Chapel, the church near Haleyville that had been built with her family's own hands.

As the family breadwinner, Mack had first been a farmer and mule trader, but then became a licensed circuit-riding Methodist minister in 1912, the third generation in his family to pursue a career in the ministry. He was appointed to the Addison Circuit and would serve six churches, which were situated in mining communities. These were very small churches, none of which could afford a minister; thus, they pooled their resources and hired Mack to attend to their spiritual needs. He would ride from one church to another each Sunday. During that first year, his salary totaled $206.19, so he continued to farm to bring in supplemental income and to feed his family. Parishioners and friends alike knew him as a very kind, caring man, who had an abundance of faith and humor. Everyone loved him. Even though it was clear that their offspring needed a whooping now and then, Mack just couldn't bring himself to do it. Thus, it became his wife's responsibility to administer discipline when the need arose.

His wife Emmett had grown up as the oldest of nine children, seven of them being boys, so she was quite accustomed to dealing with youngsters. In later years, her sister Helen declared that Emmett was twenty-five years ahead of her time—she would make as crafts things that had been unheard of then, but would later become popular. She was also a wonderful seamstress, making clothes for her family that could rival any Fifth Avenue label. Once she had had five children, Emmett wanted a family portrait taken. She got everyone dressed up in their fanciest—the girls wore little white dresses with lace and embroidery—and had the portrait taken for posterity. This had been done in their home, and Emmett hung a quilt up behind them as a backdrop. That might have been due to her creative nature or, as Hallie would later suspect, because the house might not have been very tidy.

Emmett was a wise and insightful poet, as well. Here is one that she wrote:

> So little it takes to make us glad,
> A letter, a word, a smile;
> And the load is lightened thro' the day,
> And we sing a song the while.
> A little nod from a passing friend,
> A little child's gay call,
> The lilting song of the mocking bird,
> The wind in the pine trees tall;
> Just a line from friend or loved ones,
> To say that "all is well."
> So many things can make us glad,
> More than our hearts can tell.

So little it takes to make us sad,
The letter that never came,
A frown, a sneer, a hasty look,
And the day is never the same.
Sorrows of a loved one or a friend,
A little child's cry of pain;
And the joy is taken out of the day
To never return again.
For our hearts respond to every joy,
Or they can be heavy and sad,
So little it takes to make us blue,
And so little to make us glad.

Mrs. Buttram was a very faithful and supportive wife, going with Mack as he served from church to church throughout the years. The family would move frequently, as a result. She was a highly intelligent woman and enjoyed teaching children. She was a regular volunteer teacher for their church's vacation Bible school. "She always taught us to be kind to all people," says Hallie, "even if it was somebody that we would not normally associate with." It could not have been easy for Emmett to get all the children ready to go to Sunday School and church each week, but she did it. Young people were her primary focus, and she would direct the plays put on by the church's youth and invite them to the parsonage for parties. She always had hot chocolate waiting for them.

Before Maxwell was born, his brother Corry had been struck by lightning while playing under a tree. Due to Emmett's quick thinking, he survived, but it left a permanent impression on his shaken mother. From then on, whenever a thunderstorm would occur, Emmett would bring her children together on her bed and read stories to them from *Uncle Remus* to distract them from the storm. It instilled in her children not only a love of reading, but also a fascination for speech and dialect. This would have a lasting influence on Maxwell.

Later in his life, Corry was to be struck again by lightning. What are the odds of it happening twice to the same person? Nevertheless, he lived on. Buttrams are not that easy to defeat.

With a family so large, money was a scarce commodity. Mack and Emmett instilled in their children the things that really mattered, though—faith, love, and humor. Upon these qualities could a successful, productive life be built. Each child was baptized in infancy and taken to church regularly. This legacy lived on: Family members would remain close to each other for the rest of their lives and would teach their own children the values that their parents had taught them.

In 1916, Mack was called to minister the Nauvoo Methodist Church in Nauvoo, Alabama, so that's where the family moved.

Almost from the beginning, little Maxwell seemed to be a bit different from the others. He wasn't interested in sports as his brother Gus was. Instead, he was a dreamer. In photographs, he would very rarely look at the camera. Instead, he'd be gazing into the distance. Dreaming, it seemed.

When Maxwell was almost three, the eighth child of the family was born on Easter Sunday. They named him Charles. This little fellow had a very short and sickly life, however, dying of pneumonia just a week before his second birthday. His grieving mother packed all his clothes into a trunk and kept it nearby for the rest of her life. "His little finger no more points the way," she wrote, "but beckons us on."

The evening of little Charles' death, Emmett felt moved to write this loving poem:

Since Yesterday

Where has he gone since yesterday
The friend who has left us here.
Tonight he seems so far away
Who yester-eve was near.
No map of ours on land or sea
His journeyings can trace,
We only know he's reached his home
And seen his Father's face.

And, Oh, he knows since yesterday
And he'll be learning fast;
The mists have all but cleared away
The mysteries are past.
The sun of truth he sought so long,
Unshadowed glows for him.
Nevermore the lowering cloud
Its radiance may dim.

And he has grown since yesterday
And he'll be growing still
The bonds of time and sense and space
That irked his eager will
Were dropped like shackles from the soul
In that first upward Flight.
The weary body frets no more
The spirit freed and light.

O dear familiar yesterday!
O sad and strange today!
Yet who would call the glad soul back
To rouse the resting clay?
Or who could wish that he might know
Our morrow's pain and strife
When he who here so longed to live
At last has entered Life.

– Emmett Maxwell Buttram

⇢   ⇠

To help supplement the family income, the Buttram brothers raised cotton and corn. Five-year-old Maxwell was the designated water boy. Their neighbors, who were not much better off financially, were happy to give the preacher's family surplus food and their children's outgrown clothes. These clothes were much welcomed by Maxwell's parents and would be handed down from sibling to sibling until they could no longer be worn. Pants were usually quite thin by the time they reached the youngest child. The family could not afford two sets of textbooks, so Gus was held back a year in school and Maxwell was advanced a year. That enabled the boys to share the same books and help each other with their lessons.

Maxwell wasn't crazy about school. It wasn't unusual to see him sound asleep at his desk. When the perturbed teacher interrupted his nap by asking how long he'd been sleeping, seven-year-old Maxwell responded, "I don't know. What day is this?"

During his childhood, Maxwell had wanted to be a preacher like his papa. The young boy could be seen sometimes in the woods, preaching to the trees.

At the age of eight, he was given a role in the church play. While he might not have remembered the details of that play in later years, he did remember vividly the applause. It was intoxicating. Being the preacher's son got him parts whenever he wanted them, which seemed to have been often.

Maxwell and brother Gus were very close. "We did everything together," says Gus. They laughed together, they played together, they fought together, they went to school together, and they even slept together. Maxwell had tender feelings for his three sisters, as well. Of all the siblings, it was eldest sister Peggy in whom he would confide. He knew that she loved him very much and anything he told her would be kept confidential. "He really, deep down, had a sort of shyness about him," Peggy said lovingly of her baby brother years later.

He idolized his eldest brother Johnny, who had a sparkling wit when in groups, and followed him everywhere as a child. When Johnny went off to college and pledged to a fraternity, he good-naturedly wore a cap with the word "RAT" on it. Once the initiation was over, he let his little brother have it. This was a gift that Maxwell cherished. He wore that cap constantly. Such heavy use eventually caused the leg of the "R" to fall off, and it now said "PAT." That's what the family began calling him, and Maxwell now had a nickname like everyone else. For the rest of his life, he would be known as Pat Buttram.

Chapter Two

In some family photos, everyone else would be wearing casual clothes while one brother was wearing a suit. Why? Because they had just one suit at that time, and the brothers took turns wearing it.

Pat was a born leader. Because of the frequency of the family's moves, he learned to make friends quickly. As a result, he was elected president of the church's youth group and manager of the football team, in spite of the fact that he didn't play the game himself.

In those coal-mining communities in which Pat grew up, entertainment was almost nonexistent. That was a situation that he felt needed a remedy. "Pat would organize groups and we'd put on shows; he'd be the boss, and know exactly what to do," says Hallie. They were talent shows and Hallie and her girlfriends would perform dances, complete with costumes and props. While a song was sung, it would be acted out on stage. Pat and Gus were a comedy team, with Gus being the straight man. Gus also played harmonica and guitar, and Pat served as emcee of these grand events. "We would charge and have people come and pay for it," recalls Hallie. "Not just our family. He'd involve other kids with it, too." It brought much joy to all the communities in which they performed. No more were the Buttram children the target of peers' chiding for their hand-me-down clothes and humble lifestyle. Now, they were the clever performers who dazzled their audience.

Pat was good at those things, but he was sometimes perceived as lazy at home. Performing household chores was one of his least-favorite things to do. Hallie remembers a time that it was Pat's turn to wash the dishes. He didn't do it, which greatly upset her. Before you can get a mule to do anything, the old saying goes, you must get his attention. Following that

9

philosophy, Hallie hit Pat on the forehead with a rolling pin. His head bled so much that it terrified her, and she deeply regretted having done that. Pat was none the worse for it, but the scar it left would remind him of that day for many years. Nevertheless, it didn't dampen his love for his sister.

While visiting his brother, Robert, who was now stationed at Fort McClellan, Pat entered an amateur show at the Noble Theater in Anniston for humorous reading. He walked away with second prize.

While still teenagers, Pat and Gus decided they would go into the entertainment business together, perhaps having their own radio show. Gus' musical talent and wit complemented Pat's humorous down-home banter beautifully. They made a fine team. At age seventeen, however, Gus came down with Pott's Disease, which is described as tuberculosis of the spine. The result was paralysis of his left side and almost total memory loss. He had to relearn everything he'd been taught during his five years of schooling. It took only two years for him to regain that knowledge. He still had years of physical therapy ahead of him, however, and would never be physically able to pursue a career in show business.

In the decades that followed, however, Gus would realize that he had been touched by the hand of God. His illness forced him to change his career plans, and he would someday become a minister. This experience taught him that one can sometimes most easily see the Master's plan when flat on his back.

➤   ⬅

Now that seventeen-year-old Pat had his diploma from Mortimer Jordan High School in Jefferson County, he enrolled at Birmingham-Southern College with the intent of following his father into the ministry. The Buttram family could never afford to send him to college but, fortunately, he had won a scholarship to this Methodist school.

One of Pat's classes was in speech. It was that professor who encouraged him to accept a part in the college's annual play. Pat obliged, and was given the role of Oscar Smith in William Alden Kimball's *The Heathers at Home*. He was told to act stupid. Knowing there was not just one way of looking stupid, he practiced different techniques in front of the mirror. But when the big night came and he stepped out on the stage, Pat forgot his memorized line. Instead, he winged it and ended up stealing the show.

In the audience was Steve Cisler, manager of WSGN radio there in Birmingham. Greatly impressed with Pat, Cisler immediately hired him as their early-morning comedy announcer. The station broadcasted its shows from the basement of the Tutwiler Hotel at that time.

Just the place to begin a "rags to riches" career.

→   ←

Eighteen-year-old Pat was now working as the "hillbilly announcer" for WSGN radio in Birmingham, and every Wednesday evening, he would emcee the Happy Hollow Barn Dance for his station. Soon, he was a regular on three shows each day. So good was he in this venue that Pat received another nickname - "the Pride of Winston County." The exposure was good, but the pay wasn't. He was receiving a mere six dollars per week.

With work taking so much of his time and the pay being scant, Pat had to change his lifestyle. He slept on a cot in the transmitter room and, for giving them a plug on the radio each morning, he was given a free weekly meal ticket at Cofields Café. "The station manager never knew of this deal," he wrote in a later issue of *Radio Varieties*, "but I never worried because I knew he never got up that early in the mornin.'"

Apparently, the time he spent at the radio station affected his school work quite a bit. Pat's father received this letter, written on Birmingham-Southern College letterhead:

February 6, 1934

Mr. W. M. Buttram
Dixiana, Alabama

Dear Mr. Buttram:

I note that Maxwell did a rather poor grade of work during the first semester here. Since he seems to be capable of doing much better work, I am wondering if you could suggest some way that I could inspire him to do better. As you know, he is very much interested in dramatics and I am afraid he has spent too much time in this way.

I have him on my list for special attention this semester. If you wish more frequent reports on his grades, I shall be glad to send them to you.

Hoping that Maxwell has found himself and that he will do the good work this semester that he is capable of doing, I am

> Very truly yours,
> W. E. Glenn
> Freshman Adviser

They needn't have worried. It was that very interest in dramatics that would provide Pat with a very good living later in life.

Station manager Cisler saw the potential in this young man and didn't want his local station to hold him back. He drove Pat to Chicago to audition for radio station WLS during their Chicago World's Fair coverage. This was a big-time station that, Cisler felt, would be able to give Pat the opportunities he deserved. WLS hosted a Saturday night show called the *National Barn Dance*, forerunner of the *Grand Ole Opry*. An hour of this dark-till-midnight program was broadcast nationally by NBC. It was called the *Alka-Seltzer Hour*, and it was during this hour that Pat had his on-the-air audition, which was thought by many to have been spontaneous. The theme of that night's show was "the good old days" and they had Pat do a man-on-the-street routine. Pat delighted in telling them humorous stories of life in his hometown down south. Executives and audience alike were charmed.

"They only paid him $15," sister Hallie says, "and I remember him bringing that check home and giving it to Dad."

Things would get better. When Pat had gotten back to Birmingham, he found a telegram from WLS. It was a job offer! He accepted, and it was when returning to Chicago that Pat rode in an airplane for the first time.

He and Patsy Montana would begin work at WLS on the same day. Among their coworkers at WLS were Gene Autry, Little Georgie Gobel, Smiley Burnette, Homer and Jethro, Andy Williams, the Hoosier Hotshots, Red Foley, and Rex Allen. At the time, Gobel was a teenager who played guitar and yodeled. "I guess Pat was the one who first got me thinking about comedy," he later recalled in a *TV Guide* interview, "and he was my biggest influence. We had guys in the 'Barn Dance' who'd black out their teeth and get laughs. But Pat was different—he just stood there and talked; and he had this way, even then, of making an audience believe every word he said."

This is where Pat would stay for the next thirteen years. He brought a bit of home with him, however. The plaid shirt he wore on stage had been made for him by his mother.

Soon before Pat had reported for his first day of work, fellow employee Gene Autry had gone to California to make a movie. Once that project was done, he returned to WLS. Right away, Gene liked Pat and asked if he would go on tour with him that summer. Pat agreed. It was during that tour that the men developed a strong friendship that would last for the rest of their lives. WLS, Autry felt, was a valuable training ground, the "granddaddy of country music." Its theater was on Eighth Street and Wabash.

According to Gene Autry's autobiography, *Back in the Saddle Again*, they were doing "county fairs all week and then came back to Chicago and did the 'Barn Dance' in front of a live audience of twelve hundred. We did two shows and sometimes they ran all night."

They now called Pat "the Winston County Flash." In addition to writing for the station's biweekly publication, *Stand By*, and appearing on the very popular *National Barn Dance*, Pat also had his own show. They named it Pat *Buttram's Radio School for Beginners Jes' Startin', featuring Pat and the Oshkosh Overall Boys*. This show was aired daily at 6:45 a.m. Little promotional memo notebooks were given out, advertising this show with the phrase, "Start the day with a smile."

In the studio and on the tours, Pat was perfecting his entertainment skills. Using intelligent material, but giving it a county delivery, delighted the audiences everywhere.

Thus, ended his college career.

Chapter Three

By October 1934, Pat was announcing on the 6:00–7:00 a.m. show, *Smile-A-While*; writing, directing, and playing the lead in his own show from 1:00–1:15 p.m.; and performing on the *National Barn Dance*. Of those three projects, the latter was the easiest for him because someone else was in charge. As he wrote to sister Peggy, about his quarter-hour show, "I have to write the whole fifteen minutes and then they censor it and have about ten copies made, and then we have to rehearse it about three times to get it timed to the SECOND."

He was making enough money now to buy some nice new clothes for himself, something that he rarely had as he was growing up. He also sent tuition money and some new clothes to brother Gus, who was now in college. Hard work has its compensations, for sure!

Living in the big city was quite different from back home. "The only trouble that I have is with my vittles," he wrote. "They don't have any corn bread here. They don't have any vegetables atal and what they do have I can't get them to understand me when I order. I ordered poached eggs and they brought me pork chops."

Pat was dining at a nice restaurant, in fact, when he was approached by a cute cigarette girl. Her name was Dorothy McFadden. When she wasn't working as cigarette girl, she was a stenographer. Pat wanted to see her again, so they began dating.

Each year, the station would put out a publication they called the *WLS Family Album*. In the 1935 edition of this album is a half-page photo of Pat with a caption that reveals his age as nineteen and states that he "shows philosophical tendencies suggesting many more years of age."

Pat was tired, though, and needed a break. He was given a month off and went back to Alabama to visit the family. He was, of course, welcomed home with open arms. Home was now located in Altoona, where Dad was serving as pastor.

In addition to visiting with family and friends, Pat also made some guest appearances on the local *Fred Steele's Barn Dance.* His brother John had recently assumed a managerial position at WJBY radio in Gadsden, so Pat would appear on several programs there, as well.

WLS honored Pat by putting his picture on the cover of their magazine, *Stand By,* on January 18, 1936, and inside was a full-page article on him. He was also included with the Pine Mountain Merry Makers in the music book the station put out. It begins with the autograph and photo of the eighteen members, followed by the music for fifteen down-home songs. One of these songs was written by John Lair, who seems to have gotten Pat to try his hand at songwriting, too. Published this same year was a song, "Since Nellie Got the Gong." On the cover of this sheet music, under the title, is printed "Words and Music by John Lair and Pat Butram [sic]." Sure enough, the words sound very much like Pat's. Here's the first verse:

> I had a sister Nellie, boys, and nothing else would do'er,
> But she must join the radio and be an amature.
> We stayed at home to figger out jest how to spend her dough,
> That they'd pay her for singin' songs acrost the radio.
> We planned to build a portico around the old home place,
> We aimed to lift the mortagidge and sister Minnie's face.
> Our rosy dreams is shattered now an' everthing's gone wrong.
> They ain't no joy at our house since Nellie got the gong.

➤   ◄

On August 3, 1936, a year after they had met, Pat and Dot married in Crown Point, Indiana. Why Indiana and not Chicago? After all, Dot had been born and raised in Chicago. "It was kind of like an elopement," said Hallie. Justice of the Peace John R. Krost performed the ceremony. Dot was nineteen and Pat was twenty-one.

➤   ◄

The September 1, 1936 issue of the newspaper column, "The Coal Bin," written by Henry Vance, proclaimed to its readers his disappointment. It read: "Dropped over by The Prairie Farmer Station, WLS, to see Pat Buttram, graduate comedian of WSGN in Birmingham, who has made good in a big way as a hick comedian on the air in Chicago. Unfortunately for us, however, Pat was out of town playing a road show engagement at Racine, Wis. At this season of the year the great bulk of Chicago radio performers have their busiest and best moneymaking season. State and county fairs are in their prime in this section and neighboring states right now, and there is always a heavy demand for radio stars to make personal appearances and furnish part of the entertainment over the fair circuits."

Vance's interest in Pat was a personal one. They had both worked at WSGN at the same time, so he was eager to see his friend succeed.

While Pat had the innate ability to tickle everyone's funny bone, he could be serious as well. He wrote a very informative article in WLS's *Stand By* magazine, January 29, 1938. Most of his articles back then were humorous and written in country dialect. This one wasn't. Here, he served as teacher:

Serious Side of HUMOR
by Pat Buttram

For quite a number of years now, there have been those of us who have turned to humor for a profession. Comedians or humorists, we are called. There is probably more money to be made in comedy than in any other branch of the show business—but it is also harder to make it.

A singer does not have to write his own songs, as a comedian does his own material. Then, too, after a singer sings a song once, he may use it again and again. The more it is sung, the more popular the song becomes. But listeners don't like to hear a joke that they've heard before. A comedian must have new material. That is the real work in comedy. Some take the easy way and hire a staff of writers, or "gag men," as they are called. But others of us prefer to work material up for ourselves, and believe me, that is really a job! If you don't believe it, just sit down and have someone give you a subject and try to write three jokes about it.

I often have people say to me, "You really have an easy job, only one 15-minute program a day." But they never stop to think of the four or five hours it takes to write that 15-minute program. To say nothing of the rehearsing and timing of it.

Some people ask, "Where does a comedian get his jokes?" The answer is—anywhere. A joke may come from any source. An article in the newspaper may suggest it, an incident seen on the street, a conversation, an old joke may be revamped, a friend may suggest it, a dream—yes, I have even dreamed a joke and wakened in the middle of the night and written it down. There is no telling where a joke may spring from. So if you are talking to some comedian, or humorous writer, and you suddenly see a far away gleam come in his eyes, you know that he has suddenly thought of a good snappy joke with which to end that routine on next week's program.

After the comedian has assembled enough gags, or jokes, to fill a 15-minute of a half-hour program, his work still isn't over. He can always depend on some of his best jokes being marked out by a program director, or the advertising agency, or by the sponsor himself. This is done for various reasons. Some jokes are against station policies. Some, the advertising agency doesn't consider funny. And I have even had a joke taken out because the name used in it was the same as that of the sponsor's sister. Although most of the censoring is done for the best, there is nothing that makes a comedian feel worse than the cutting and changing of his script.

Then, after a script is OK'd and rehearsed, there is still the question of how the public will receive it. A joke is either funny or silly. There is no way of telling how the public will take it. I always try them out on my wife first. If she laughs at a joke, it must be good. If there is a studio audience, it's easy to tell if the material is going over or not. But if there isn't, we just have to wait for the fan mail.

A comedian has another price to pay for his position. At any party or with any group, he is always expected to be funny. He must always have a funny answer for everything that is asked him. If a listener talks to him, everything he says is expected to be funny. He must always portray the same character that he plays on the air. For that reason, I stay away from parties and dodge listeners. This makes me "stuck-up," in their estimation, but if I did talk to them, and didn't say things that were funny, then they'd say that I am a fake—that I am not natural at all, but can only be funny when I am reading jokes from a script.

In these few paragraphs I have only told the hard side of a comedian's work. There is a lot of happiness in the work, as there is in all work. The fact that I've made other people laugh, made other people happy, more than repays me for any trouble I may have had doing it. So the next time you listen to a comedy program, and you hear the comedian use one old joke and eight new ones, don't turn off the radio and say, "He just pulled the oldest joke I ever heard." But instead, say, "He just pulled eight of the newest jokes I ever heard."

His monthly column, "Whittlin's," appeared now in not only WLS's magazine, but also in the *Rural Radio* magazine. These columns consisted of random musings, written in dialect. Here's a compilation of his best ones:

WHITTLIN'S

Don't go around with yer nose up in th' air. People mite think ye kan't afford a handerchief.

Why do men spend three dollars fer a shirt an' then cover all but a nickel's worth uv it with a coat an' vest?

Money does talk...It'll say goodbye awful easy.

About th' greatest water power that I know uv is a woman's tears.

Th' only shore way to git rid uv a enemy is t' make a friend out uv him.

It's bad enuf to be a quitter but it's worse not to even begin.

If opertunity knocks at yore door...open it. But be shore ye shut th' back door first.

I read th' other day wher ye kin hear better with yer eyes shut. I hav often noticed people trying this out in church.

A committee is a body of men that keeps minutes and wastes hours.

Yourn til they put zippers on string beans,

– PAT

Pat would be featured often in "The Coal Bin." On June 21, 1938, news about him took two columns. Pat had been paying another yearly visit to his home state and the newspaper, and Vance found him not much changed from his WSGN days. The big time hadn't spoiled him. Except for one thing: "Pat seems to have acquired the bait of wearing fancy breeches while in Chicago, and he had on one of those plaid coat arrangements which was a knockout. As I understand it, he's mighty busy during the Fall season with personal appearance stuff in the rural precincts of the Midwest. I betcha Pat adopts a different style of dress from what he is now wearing when he hits the whistle stops and does the county fair humor, reserving the double-breasted plaids and the ice cream pants for the folks back home."

Republic Pictures had offered him a part in a movie, with Elviry and the Weaver Brothers, due to begin production that autumn. Pat didn't know whether to accept or not. WLS was providing him with steady employment and a regular paycheck. Should he trade that for a chance at Hollywood? Sure, Hollywood would pay better, but it's certainly not very secure employment. He decided to be content with what he had and declined the offer.

Pat's on-air work as the rural humorist on the *National Barn Dance* was enjoyed, but it was not a major role. He almost always wrote his own material, the exception being when he could recite lighthearted poems that fellow Alabaman Luther Patrick wrote for him. The two men developed a close friendship that would endure for the rest of Luther's life, and Patrick would go on to become a congressman. He was the composer of a poem, "Sleepin' at the Foot o' the Bed," which Buttram would often quote during these early years. This, many people felt, was Luther's masterpiece. Pat agreed.

SLEEPIN' AT THE FOOT O' THE BED

Did ye ever sleep at the foot o' the bed
  When the weather wuz whizzin' cold,
When the wind wuz a'whistlin' aroun' the house
  An' the moon wuz yeller ez gold,
An' give yore good warm mattress up
  To Aunt Lizzie and Uncle Fred,
Too many kinfolks on a bad, raw night
  And you went to the foot o' the bed –
  Fer some dern reason the coldest night o' the season
An' you wuz sent to the foot o' the bed?

I could allus wait till the old folks et
  An' then eat the leavin's with grace,
The teacher could keep me after school
  An' I'd still hold a smile on my face,
I could wear the big boys' wore-out clothes
  Er let sister have my sled,
But it allus did git my nanny goat
  To have to sleep at the foot o' the bed –
  They's not a location top side o' creation
That I hate like the foot o' the bed.

'Twuz fine enough when kinfolks come,
  The kids brought brand new games,
You could see how fat all the old folks wuz
  An' learn all the babies' names,
Had biscuits an' custard an' chicken pie,
  Allus got Sunday fed,
But you knowed dern well when night come on
  You wuz headed for the foot o' the bed;
  You couldn't get by it, they wuz no use to try it,
You wuz set fer the foot o' the bed.

—Luther Patrick

Back at home, there seemed to be something missing. Dot was unable to bear children of her own, but wanted very badly to adopt a child. Pat was agreeable. At the time, Tennessee's adoption laws were not as stringent as many others, so the couple went to the Tennessee Children's Home in Memphis and chose the baby they wanted. They weren't able to take her home right away, however, because she developed an illness that required hospitalization for a couple months.

Once she was theirs, they took her home, named her Gayle Patricia (in honor of her new daddy), and showered her with love.

❧   ❧

Pat might not have always had a major role in *National Barn Dance* (although he was often its master of ceremonies), but he was definitely noticed. In the April 22, 1940 edition of the *Sheboyken Press*, it was said that "Buttram will be one of the most fortunate of all radio performers on the air when television becomes a reality. This slow-spoken Alabaman is a true stage performer and even when working in a broadcasting studio acts his lines out as though he were before an audience." That's not surprising. Pat was, after all, just being himself.

Some of Pat's humor was now being quoted quite often by other people. This one showed up in the newspaper: "Middle age has arrived when you have the choice of two temptations—and you take the one that gets you home earlier."

It was considered quite prestigious to be an employee of WLS. It also gave Pat the advantage of working near his sister, Hallie, whose military husband was now stationed in the Chicago area. He stayed with them for a full two weeks once, "and we had a great visit," she says.

Chapter Four

Radio Varieties **asked Pat** to write a two-page autobiographical article, and it ran in their March 1941 issue. After giving a truthful, but humorous, accounting of his life thus far, he wrote, "For the benefit of all the girls I'll describe myself. I have my father's black hair, my mother's brown eyes and my brother's green pants. I am five feet ten an' one half inches tall an' weigh a hundred and eighty pounds soakin' wet. If I keep on gainin' I'll look like a bail of hay with the middle hoop busted. I am twenty five years old and have got rhumatism already. I am number 1065 in the draft regerstration."

Henry Vance wrote about Pat again in "The Coal Bin," the Friday, May 9, 1941 edition. This time, Pat's homecoming rated three columns of coverage. "Buttram is a pretty good example of what happens to a fellow who sticks everlastingly at it, and who insists on having a one-track mind in so far as a career is concerned," he wrote. "He manfully swallowed the bitter pills, long after the original sugar-coating had worn off, bided his time and waited his chance." He continues, "Today the lad who used to be mighty close akin to a dollar-a-year man down at WSGN is one of the top-billing stars of the NBC network that goes out over the air each Saturday night." Pat was now taking the place on the *National Barn Dance* of Uncle Ezra, who had been a humorous fixture for some time. This was a big advancement. Now that Ezra had left, Pat was the top comic, appearing regularly on the show, rather than sporadically. Things were looking good for him.

On his next trip back home, Pat talked his parents into coming to Chicago. There was so much to see and so much to do in such a big city. He wanted to show them everything.

Pat's mother was doing more traveling now than usual. She also went to Florida to help her sister, but became ill while there. Her ailment was later diagnosed as ovarian cancer. Pat and Gus would visit home frequently during their mother's illness.

In September of the same year, Pat was given another three columns in "The Coal Bin." Vance had decided to go to Chicago himself so he could see Pat at work. Alas, the cast and crew were packing for a run over to Indianapolis, where that week's show would be broadcast. Pat tried to get him to go along with them, but Vance had to decline.

Pat's sister Hallie and her family were living in Indiana now, so they came to the show. "I was three or so," recalls Hallie's daughter Harriet. "They got me up on the stage and asked what those little things were that light up. They were lightnin' bugs." The visiting Chicagoans got a kick out of little Harriet's southern drawl. "I got a dollar for that and bought a rubber doll with it that I had wanted so much." Pat enjoyed his little niece and took pictures of her whenever he could. She was an easy child to love because she was so well mannered.

Once Pat and company got back to Chicago the following Sunday, he gave Vance a call at the hotel and invited him to the rodeo and thrill show at Soldier Field. The men and their wives had the best seats, and enjoyed this well-attended event.

Later that week, Pat had a show to do in Wisconsin. This time of year, he was very busy with personal appearances around the country and would take his little family with him.

"I remember traveling all over the country with my parents when I was very little, being in forty-two of the then-forty-eight states before I was three years old," recalls Gayle. "At about three, I remember Daddy bringing me out on stage and putting me on Gene's horse, Champion. I guess that's where my love of horses began."

As soon as an engagement was over, they would return home—many times at 3:00 a.m. Home at that time was in the Chicago Heights area. Even when they had gotten back in during the wee hours of the morning, Pat would still show up at work the next morning at the usual time.

"At one time," Gayle continues, "we lived in the Knickerbocker Hotel for a while. I thought I was pretty smart because I could call room service and order whatever I wanted. However, I always ordered two sundaes, malts, or whatever. You see, I had an elderly lady babysitting me and she was always included in my order. Little did I know that my folks were down in the dining room approving my orders with the staff. There was also a bellhop who occasionally brought me a chocolate bar when he had to come up to our floor for something."

➤   ◄

The Birmingham News-Age-Herald announced, on December 21, 1941, that Pat had been named the "official tree climber" for the Possum Hunters Club. How appropriate, he thought. "Oxanna is in Winston County, right in the middle of 'possum country,'" he told them.

That same day would bring about an event that would result in a very bleak Christmas for the whole Buttram family. Their mother, whose cancer had metastasized, died. How Pat wished he could have given her a life of luxury, as he knew she deserved. The sadness he felt for his mother never went away.

While home, Pat saw that brother Gus' back and leg ailments were getting so bad that he wasn't able to get around much. He took him to Chicago and had specialists check him out. They did a wonderful job. They improved Gus' quality of life considerably.

During his convalescence, Gus was able to attend a *National Barn Dance* show. He was given one of the choicest seats in the house, right near the stage. "Just to sorter get Pat's reaction to a bit of silent heckling," he told reporter Henry Vance, "I tossed a penny on the stage. Pat stopped his routine long enough to pick up the copper, stick it into his pocket, and remark extemporaneously, 'You can always tell a skunk by the cent he throws!'"

➤   ◄

The *WLS Family Album* for 1943 ran a third-page photo of Pat with a caption that said, "You might not ever find it out, but Pat is a highly intelligent and well educated young man, son of a circuit riding preacher. He really did come from Winston County, Alabama, and he really does talk most of the time the same way he does on the stage or on the radio. He was just born with a comical streak."

In that same year, Pat was featured in his very first movie. Called *National Barn Dance*, it was the video version of the radio show and included the players that had made the radio show such a rousing success. All the favorites were there—Pat, Lulubelle and Scotty, and the Hoosier Hotshots.

This brought him to the attention of Louella Parsons, who mentioned him in her August 28 column. She wrote, "Funny thing how promising new film personalities are through the grapevine before they even appear on the screen. Take Pat Buttram, of whom I confess I knew little or nothing. He makes his screen debut in 'National Barn Dance,' which Walter MacEwen produced at Paramount. Now several companies have bids in for Pat, who is a new face with a unique voice that sounds off with homespun humor. It is so difficult to get really good comedians that it looks as if Pat is in."

One of the bids might have been from 20th Century-Fox, for the remake of *State Fair*. There was talk about putting Pat in the role that Will Rogers had had previously in 1933. This deal apparently fell through, however. (Charles Winninger played the role in the 1945 release.)

In the meantime, his WLS work continued. In 1945, the station put out the *Happy-Go-Lucky Almanak*, in which Pat had the "Advice to the Luvlorn" column. In his byline, he was credited as "Pat Buttram, D.D., P.H.D., and LSMFT." (A reference to the cigarette company's catch phrase, "Lucky Strike means fine tobacco.") Here is an example of the questions and answers in this hilarious column:

Dear Mr. Buttram: I am getting married next month and my girlfriend says she will never stop loving me, that we will go on billing and cooing forever. Do you think I can believe her?
Signed, Lovesick

Dear Lovesick: Don't worry about it. The cooing may only last till the end of the honeymoon, but the billing will go on forever.
Perfessor Buttram.

According to the *Academy Players Directory #41*, published that year, Pat was being represented by Helen Ainsworth of the National Concert and Artists Corporation. He was listed as an emcee of *National Barn Dance*, as seen on NBC.

Pat and his family now moved into a house on Coldwater Canyon in California. "I remember spending many, many happy hours with my dad there," Gayle says. "He was a really loving and caring father."

Her parents' marriage, however, had become quite rocky. They decided to divorce. Once they parted, Dot would not allow Pat to see their six-year-old daughter anymore.

According to family members, the divorce was a bitter one.

⇥   ⇤

Roy Rogers expressed interest in Pat for his sidekick, but, as he already had multiple sidekicks, another wasn't needed. Pat did make a few appearances on Rogers' radio show, however, beginning in 1946.

After many offers, the winner for Pat's services would be an old friend from WLS.

The humble home in which Pat was born. [From the collection of Hallie Reed.]

The Buttram children, from left to right: Corry, Hallie, Gus, Peggy holding baby Pat, Mamie, and Johnny. [From the collection of Zella Fuller.]

This time, it was Pat's turn to wear the suit. [From the collection of Hallie Reed.]

Mr. and Mrs. Pat Buttram.
[Courtesy of WLS radio.]

"Perfesser Buttram" points to the sweetest spot on earth, Alabama.
[Courtesy of WLS radio.]

Pat with some of the *National Barn Dance* cast [Courtesy of WLS radio.]

Publicity shot of Pat.
[Courtesy of WLS radio.]

...and now they are
three. Little Gayle is her
parents' pride and joy.
[Courtesy of WLS radio.]

Robert Benchley was Pat's friend and mentor.
[From the collection of Kerry Galgano.]

No one could keep a straight face with Pat around. [Courtesy of WLS radio.]

The whole gang at WLS. That's Pat sitting in the front-middle.

Pat wasn't a sidekick in his first Gene Autry movie. That would
come later. [From the collection of Kerry Galgano.]

Jody Gilbert, Gregg Barton, Gene Autry, Richard Emory, and
Pat in *Gene Autry and the Mounties*. [From the collection of
Kerry Galgano. Photo by Walters, Columbia Pictures.]

Columbia's "Valley of Fire"—Pat Buttram, Gene Autry &
Terry Frost [Courtesy of Gene Autry Entertainment]

Sidekick Pat is spooked in *Wagon Team*.

Gene Autry, Sheila Ryan, and Pat in *Mule Train* [from the collection of Kerry Galgano.]

Another scene from *Mule Train*. [from the collection of Kerry Galgano.]

Another scene from *Mule Train*. [from the collection of Kerry Galgano.]

Beautiful Sheila was already an established actress. She had appeared with Lloyd Bridges in the Republic film *Hideout*. [From the collection of Kerry Galgano.]

With Smiley Burnette in *Pack Train*. [From the collection of Kerry Galgano.]

Chapter Five

Pat liked it in California. He had been hired to be on Phil
Harris' radio show. The two men had a disagreement, however: Phil
wanted to Hollywoodize Pat's name; Pat wanted to keep it just the way it
was. They soon parted company professionally, but not personally. The
two men would remain good friends for life.

Considered the first successful singing movie cowboy, Gene Autry
was working steadily in Hollywood, making a series of popular films, and
doing radio. One thing that set his movies apart from the usual Western
fare was that his portrayed women as spunky and independent, and Autry's character was always a gentleman, even when in a fight. While he
served in the military during World War II, however, his former sidekick,
Smiley Burnette, had been assigned by Republic to work with Roy Rogers.
Autry had returned to civilian life and began making pictures again, so
Sterling Holloway served as his sidekick for one picture and Johnny Bond,
of the Cass County Boys singing trio, had been filling in since then. Gene
needed an actor who would provide permanent comic relief to his films,
however. He had noticed Pat's appearances on some of Roy Rogers' radio
shows and remembered him from their WLS days. He really liked Pat, so
he asked him to come work for him. Pat happily agreed.

"Nobody [who worked for Autry] had a contract," says Johnny Western. "His handshake was better than anybody else's paper." The only time
actual contracts were signed in Western's memory was for the movies,
and that was only because the Screen Actors Guild required it. Gene Autry was a man of the highest integrity and his employees knew it.

By September, Pat was under contract to appear in six films a year
with Autry. It would be hard work—often shooting two pictures at the

same time, but very rewarding. Their first film together, *The Strawberry Roan*, was released in 1948. This would be the first of only two color films that Autry made. Pat wasn't a sidekick in this film but, rather, the role was more like his appearances on *National Barn Dance*. He played a hired hand named Hank. He would later evolve into the ever-present sidekick.

The Strawberry Roan was shot in Sedona, Arizona, and told the story of Champion coming into Gene Autry's life. This beautiful horse would usually get second billing to the star in the opening credits. Introduced in this picture was Little Champ, otherwise known as Champion, Jr.

Pat was eight years younger than Gene, but the show's decision-makers wanted him to appear older. He was clean-shaven in *The Strawberry Roan*, but was soon asked to grow whiskers. Pat complied. His image would be intentionally less polished than Autry's and quite unsophisticated. That worked well with his voice and style of humor.

He did quite a few of his own stunts in those days. In the book, *Those Great Cowboy Sidekicks*, by David Rothel, Pat tells why: "When I first started with Autry, I knew Buster Keaton very well. I went out and talked with him, and he showed me how to do some falls. He said, 'If it's possible to do a stunt in comedy yourself, do it—in a water trough, a cactus, or wherever you're to fall.' He said, 'It's not the fall that gets the laugh; it's your reaction as you hit the ground or whatever, and then getting up. If they have to cut to a double and then cut back to you for your reaction, it's not as effective as if it's one big take.' Keaton also said, 'There's going to be kids watching your picture, so when you fall get up real quick because if kids think you're hurt, they won't laugh. When they see you're okay, then they'll laugh like hell.' He helped me a lot."

There were times, though, when stuntmen were needed. "I'm an old stuntman," says Whitey Hughes, who worked on many Autry projects over the years. "Been fifty-six years in the business. I worked with all of them—I worked with Gabby Hayes, I worked with Andy Clyde, I worked with—you name their sidekicks and I have worked with them. I never met a more down-to-earth, likeable man than Pat Buttram. He was one of the funniest sidekicks." Hughes gives an example of what a good businessman Autry was. "Gene gave Pat an open road because he wasn't afraid of the sidekick upstaging him. He just told Pat, 'Be as funny as you can be because it makes the ratings better.'"

Roy Flynn, Chair of Radio and English at Florida State, Tallahassee, and also the son-in-law of Pat's sister Peggy, told reporters that Pat was writing the entire Gene Autry scripts now, both the comedy for his character and the dramatics for the rest of the cast. "The drama part of the show has been giving Pat quite a bit of trouble," he said, "but thus far he has been able to come through with colors flying." This was apparently relative to Autry's radio show titled *Melody Ranch*. Pat would be a part of this show until its final broadcast in 1956.

Melody Ranch had something for everyone. Gene and the Cass County Boys provided the vocal music, with about five songs interspersed throughout the half-hour show. Then Gene would be straight-man for Pat's comedy sketch. "Patrick" and "Mr. Artery" (as they called each other) played well off each other. A little while later, they would act out the much-more-serious story of the day. "Pat brought to *Melody Ranch* a fresh and new brand of comedy, but he's been in the entertainment business a long time, in spite of the fact he's a very young man," wrote Kathleen Lamb in the show's souvenir program. "A natural mimic and comedian, Pat began, as an amateur, 'taking off' some of the rustic town characters. His mimicry was kindly and considerate. He never makes any hill-billy an object of ridicule; rather does he try to endear his homespun personalities to an audience. That is the reason, even in country towns and rural villages, Pat Buttram is always a welcome entertainer." Regarding his relationship with show regular Johnny Bond, she wrote, "Each is a perfect foil for the other, and between them, Buttram with his long-winded Dixie drawling dialogue, and Bond with his pungent Oklahoma twang have concocted so many unpredictable situations on the *Melody Ranch* program, as to make the patient 'Mister Ar-tery' wince when he sees them coming." Off stage, Pat didn't look the way he sounded, however. "He is nearly always unrecognized by the *Melody Ranch* fans who storm stage doors seeking out their favorites. Pat's raucous voice becomes a quiet, Southern speech of Alabama, and his masculine, husky frame fits excellently into his impeccably tailored 'eastern' clothes in the New York manner. Paradoxically, Pat, in private life, is the Dude of Melody Ranch."

The days of brothers taking turns wearing the same suit were long gone.

Gene was grateful for Pat's contribution to the success of his show. The budget was modest, and it seemed to Autry's business manager that Buttram was always asking for a raise, but he did get paid well enough to do some investing. According to the February 21, 1949 "The Coal Bin," Pat was now part-owner of the Haleyville radio station.

Buttram had just finished making the 1949 Autry film, *Riders in the Sky,* when he received word that his beloved father was ill, so he hastened to Alabama to be with him. Fortunately, the elder Buttram recovered and all was well.

Pat then returned to work. These Westerns would often be filmed in Pioneertown for several reasons. Situated about 150 miles from Los Angeles near Palm Springs, Pioneertown was built to mimic a town from the old west. Cacti and rock formations were abundant. The weather was good. A street had been permanently constructed to look like that of a typical western town of yore. The street had been made wide enough for a stagecoach to turn around, perhaps for scenes to be reenacted for tourists, but it wasn't conducive to filmmaking. Nevertheless, the Autry company spent an entire summer there and a hundred of their television shows were made in that location. Because of the over-wideness of the street, however, we wouldn't usually see it in its entirety on screen; we saw only a corner or a storefront at a time.

The street was too wide, but the water trough was too narrow. That's what Pat would remember most about this location. As the sidekick, it seemed almost a given that he'd end up in the water trough sooner or later in most episodes. Its narrowness caused him many a scrape.

"He was just *so funny!*" recalls Johnny Western. "Gene loved to set it up. He loved to watch Buttram work just so he could laugh."

The cast and crew stayed at the Golden Stallion Motel during that summer. For a day or so every week, Pat and Gene would fly back to town to do their radio show.

Dozens of Autry movies were made. The one that stands out from all the rest to Pat was *Mule Train*, which was filmed at the Alabama Hills in Lone Pine, California. The scenery there was beautiful, and the cameramen took full advantage of it, getting gorgeous shots. The movie seems to have greatly impressed other people, too. The Museum of Modern Arts in New York voted it the best B-western of all time. It humanized the history of the discovery of cement in the west. Buttram fans loved it, too. To them, it was a treat to see him, rather than The Singing Cowboy, singing the title song in the first scene and getting so much screen time. This short scene took half a day to film. Why? Because mules aren't known for their easy compliance. Just because the script called for Pat to lead the mules across the prairie while he sang the song was no guarantee that the animals wanted to be led. Finally, in order to get this scene shot, two prop men had to get behind the six mules and throw pebbles at them— not enough to hurt them, but just enough to make them move forward. Their method worked *too* well. The mules practically ran over Pat. They finally got the scene done to the director's satisfaction, and then it became official—Pat Buttram was the first person to ever sing the song "Mule Train" for the public. Many singers would record it in the future—Frankie Laine, Tennessee Ernie Ford, Burl Ives, etc.—but Pat was the first. This, he felt, was one of his best roles ever.

As Pat told writer David Rothel, "*Mule Train* shows you the character of Gene Autry, to let a guy come in and just take the whole part—it's *my* picture; it's the sidekick's picture for a change. Gene just encouraged it and helped out all he could to see that it held up as a picture rather than trying to hog it all for himself. A lot of guys in Westerns, if the sidekick happened to get a little ahead of the star on his horse—now this is no joke—the star would stop the scene and say, 'You get back; I want to be six feet ahead.' This was often the rule of a lot of them, but Autry wasn't that way at all."

Others, too, feel that this film was exceptional. Columbia University, in fact, deemed it an example of how good B Westerns can be. "It is in the library in New York City," Pat told Rothel, "as the best B Western ever made."

Something else made this picture especially significant to Pat, too. A beautiful dark-haired actress named Sheila Ryan played the female lead, and she stole Pat's heart.

Six years his junior, Sheila had been acting for about ten years. Hollywood had succeeded with her, where it had failed with Pat. "Sheila Ryan" was only her professional name. The name she was given at birth was Catherine Elizabeth McLaughlin. This lovely lady had been married twice; very briefly to actors Allan "Rocky" Lane and Edward Norris, but was now single again.

It was a small world—back in 1943, Sheila had worked with her friend Alice Faye (wife of Pat's friend Phil Harris) in the Twentieth Century-Fox movie *The Gang's All Here.*

Sheila would change Pat's life forever.

Chapter Six

Once *Mule Train* **had wrapped,** it was time to go on the road. *The Birmingham News* announced, with much fanfare, that Gene Autry and his co-stars, including his horses Champion and Champion, Jr., would be visiting Birmingham on Thursday, March 9, 1950. The shows would begin at 4:00 and 8:15. They were being sponsored by the Birmingham Chamber of Commerce for the benefit of the athletic fund. Their first goal was to raise some funds for the Boys Industrial School's gym.

The troupe, which also included Smiley Burnett, was welcomed to town by a very familiar face—Madelaine Beatty, who had worked on the Autry show in the past and was now in Birmingham to visit her grandparents.

"My first recollection of Uncle Pat was when he came with Gene Autry to do a 'wild west' show at what is now Boutwell Auditorium in Birmingham," says Gus' son Mac. "The local NBC affiliate, WABT Channel 13, had a show that was somewhat like today's noontime news broadcast—a lot of local events. My sister Mary and I were invited to be guests on the show preceding the Gene Autry show coming to Birmingham. TV was very new to everyone, especially to us since there was not one in our home. As we were being interviewed, Mary did most of the talking. I was so amazed because I could see myself on the studio monitor, but couldn't quite grasp that the image I saw was me, and it was me on TV and me in person. So I spent most of the time moving my hands from behind my head to into my pockets, just watching myself."

When the television appearance was over, Mac went to the Autry show and was ushered backstage to see the stars. He was thrilled to meet

Autry and Champion. "Most little boys back then wanted to be cowboys, and there I was with my favorite cowboy and his sidekick, my Uncle Pat."

Other guests during the early performance were all the Alabama 4-H Clubs presidents. These boys and girls were given the royal treatment; they, too, met the stars in person backstage. The photo that appeared in *The Birmingham News* soon afterward showed both Gene and Pat happily signing their autographs for Winfield 4-H'er Joe Hubbard.

This Birmingham stop was the sixteenth day of a nationwide tour, which consisted of one- or two-day stands. Such a tour was grueling for all the players and crew, but for Pat it was even more difficult. He had the flu and was running a temperature of 101.5. He carried out his comic routine in his usual professional manner, however, with no one the wiser.

"The Coal Bin" columnist, Henry Vance, visited Pat backstage too, and he was quite surprised to find that his old friend now had whiskers. In Vance's resulting article, he included a poem that was inspired by this revelation:

> Mr. Buttram's not afeared
> > To grow chin whiskers or a beard,
> Or tremble lest this birdie's nest
> > Would by smoking fag be seared.

There were three young children who wanted so badly to attend the show, but couldn't. Two of them were in iron lungs—polio victims. Gene went to them at the polio ward at Jefferson-Hillman Hospital. After that, they went to the Crippled Children's Clinic. It seems that stars of his ilk felt a responsibility to their fans, to set a good example for them and to show them they cared.

⇥   ⇤

Gene Autry: "What is the Buttram plan to do away with income tax?"
Pat Buttram: "Mass unemployment."

Gene made sure that unemployment would not be a problem for Pat. In addition to their many movies, the two men were now working on *The Gene Autry Show* series for television. This highly-successful series would run from 1950 until 1956. Pat was kept quite busy with all these projects, but Gene, being the star who appeared in most scenes, was even busier. It worried Pat that Gene was pushing himself so hard, but his concern didn't slow the man down.

➤   ◄

Sidekicks are essential in the world of showbiz. Pat would later explain to *Chicago Daily News* reporter Bob Rose how the term came about. "Dr. Watson was one of the first sidekicks. In fact the term came from his country," he said. "The 'kick' refers to a pocket. The back pocket was the favorite target of pickpockets, but the side pocket or 'sidekick' was considered safe, dependable and reliable. So a guy you could trust became a sidekick."

According to Autry's autobiography, Pat teamed up with Andy Devine to establish a club called The Exalted Order of Sidekicks. Jay Silverheels and William Frawley were among its many members. This lighthearted club lobbied unsuccessfully for the following perks:

1) When a sidekick is thrown into a water trough, the water must be heated.
2) Pies thrown into the face of a sidekick must come from the bar of the Brown Derby.
3) The sidekick gets the girl in every tenth picture.
4) The sidekick must be reimbursed for money he has loaned the star.
5) The sidekick must be reimbursed for coffee he has purchased to sober up members of the cast, including himself.

"Everywhere he went," says fellow actor Bill Hale, "he [Pat] made people laugh. Just to look at him made you laugh."

The Autry troupe worked fast in the 1950s, usually filming two movies at the same time, while also doing their weekly TV and radio shows. After a while, it became evident that Gene was having difficulty remembering from one set to the next what Pat's current character's name was. This necessitated many retakes. Thus, they decided to let both Gene and Pat use their real names in these projects. Problem solved.

➤   ◄

Lovely actress Donna Martell was on the *Hills of Utah* movie set when she met Pat for the first time. They were sitting between takes with some time to spare, so he got his script out. His script cover was quite unusual. "It was the prettiest one I had ever seen," she says. "In the business, I'd seen many, but it was beautiful. It was a golden brown and etched in gold. His name was prominent in gold letters." She admired it and told him so.

Much to her surprise, he came to work the very next day with another one just like his, only this new one had Donna's name on it. "I almost fainted!" she exclaims. "I was so excited. Through my entire career, that is the script holder that I used."

⇀ ↽

Early in September of 1950 Pat came very close to death.

It was reported in many different ways, often contradictory, in newspapers. What really happened? A few months later, Pat wrote a letter about it to his friend Luther Patrick, who shared it with "The Coal Bin" reporter, Henry Vance. Here, in part, is what it said: "I guess you heard about the accident, but there are so many garbled reports going around that I wanted to give you the straight dope so you can tell it to all of my relatives who come into town on Saturday afternoon.

"We were making a Gene Autry movie up at Pioneertown, about 35 miles from Twentynine Palms. I was standing beside a brass cannon which I was supposed to shoot into the air for the purpose of rainmaking. The cannon, which was supposedly loaded with non-explosive flash powder, exploded, filling me with pieces of shrapnel and cutting a gash across my chest a foot long and about four inches wide. My right lung was punctured, my chin cut open, and an artery in my left leg severed."

An additional injury, one that would be with him for the rest of his life, was the loss of sight in one eye. It would be diagnosed as a detached retina, but was apparently unfixable.

Gene and crew members who were nearby had only minor injuries.

Pat, said Autry in his autobiography, was not mechanically inclined and had always been leery of machines. According to this book, it was a television show they were filming at the time. While movies had strict rules, television was new and those rules had not been adopted yet for small-screen productions. They weren't required to have a licensed professional doing the explosives, so it became the domain of the prop men. Big mistake!

Pat knew that the injury to his leg needed immediate attention and kept trying to tell them that, but it was an unseen peril, covered by his boot. Gene, trying to be helpful, kept shushing him, trying to get him to lie still and be quiet.

The company's plane was at the local airport several miles away. They put Pat in a pickup truck, with Gene beside him, and rushed him to the airstrip. Pat was barely conscious at this point. "There was literally a hole in his chest," wrote Autry, "and you could see his lungs, and part of his chin was blown off." Pilot Herb Green urged them to bring a doctor to Pat to stabilize him before attempting to fly him anywhere. They would get Dr. Bill Ince, son of Dr. Tom Ince, for whom a hospital was named. Green flew to Twentynine Palms to fetch the doctor. In the meantime, they carried Pat from the truck into the small office nearby. As they awaited the doctor's arrival, Gene kept reassuring Pat, trying to keep him from going into shock. After a while, he realized it would be getting dark soon, so Gene told the phone operator they needed to light up the runway for the doctor. The operator called all over town, and it was even announced at the local baseball game. The response was immediate: plenty of people brought their cars, lined them up along the runway, and turned their headlights on.

When Dr. Ince arrived and saw how critically injured Pat was, he felt it was inadvisable to administer any drugs that would lessen the pain. While he was working, pilot Green flew two more errands—to fetch some blood plasma and an assisting doctor. Dr. Ince had Pat's wounds cleaned and stitched before the ambulance got there.

The ambulance driver looked at Pat, then tried to put Gene into the ambulance.

"No," said Gene, "you take him," indicating Pat.

"He's gone, Mister," replied the driver.

Gene was adamant. "*You take him!*" There was no way he was going to leave his friend there to die.

Feeling he had no choice, the driver put Pat into the ambulance. Gene got in with him. Not only was Pat gravely injured, but he was also in shock, in spite of Autry's efforts to prevent it. During the drive to Thomas H. Ince Memorial Hospital in Twentynine Palms, Gene kept talking and talking to Pat, doing everything he could to keep him awake.

When they arrived at the hospital, Pat was immediately taken to the operating room. Anesthesia was administered, but he refused to go to sleep. Feeling sure that he would die if he so much as closed his eyes, he tried his best to stay conscious. He had so much to live for—his family, his girlfriend, his career. He didn't want to die. It took a massive dose to finally put him out.

It was a very long surgery. He required four blood transfusions, with more scheduled.

While Gene was waiting and praying, he went to the phone and called Sheila. Without hesitation, she packed a suitcase, loaded up her cat, and drove out into the night to be by Pat's side. She registered at the Dow Motel, prepared to stay for however long he needed her.

When he came out of surgery, he was put on the critical list. The doctor gave him a fifty-fifty chance of survival.

When Pat's family in Alabama learned of the accident, they were very, very worried. Gus' daughter Mary was six years old at the time. She says, "I remember knowing that he was injured and Daddy going into the front bedroom and praying until he thought Uncle Pat was going to be okay. I remember Daddy crying and being upset."

Prayer can move mountains. By September 14, it was announced to the press that Pat would recover. Divine intervention, the best care that money could buy, the loving attention of Sheila, and his strong determination had all worked together to pull him through.

Pat's ex-wife Dot's feelings softened. She and her mother took little Gayle to see Pat at the hospital. "I think I was about eight or nine years old then," Gayle recalls. Knowing ahead of time that he would be seeing his little girl again, Pat arranged to have a gift waiting for her. "He gave me a cowgirl outfit, and I was the proudest little girl around. That's the only time I can remember [my parents] seeing each other after the divorce."

On Saturday night, December 2, Pat returned to *The Gene Autry Show*, receiving a big welcome. This must have been a cameo appearance, however, perhaps meant to reassure their fans, because Autry's autobiography states that Pat was out of work for nine months because of his injuries.

He still spent much time at the hospital. His recovery would take many months. "The result is that I expect to be completely discharged from here about the first of the year," Pat wrote in the letter that was included in "The Coal Bin" column. "I am able to get around pretty well now and the wounds are practically all healed.

"Gene has been really swell about everything. He has kept me on full salary during my illness, and of course the insurance company is taking care of the hospital bills. Gene is going on another personal appearance tour in January which will take him through Birmingham, and I am just hoping that I'll be well enough by then to go along."

When asked if the nurses had had him under observation, he responded, "Oh, yes, and vice versa."

Pat's sense of humor was still alive and well.

There was a side effect of this accident that would cause an unforeseen inconvenience in the future: Because of the shrapnel that remained in his body, Pat would always set off the metal detectors in airports.

The project they were filming when the accident happened was shelved for a while, then was resurrected for a later episode, "The Peacemaker," in which Chill Wills was the one firing the small cannon. During Pat's many months of recuperation, Wills, Alan Hale, Jr. ("Tiny"), and Fuzzy Knight ("Sagebrush") filled in for him on the television show, usually wearing the same outfit that Pat did.

Decades later, his daughter would say, "For years after that, whenever anyone asked Dad what he had learned from working in the movie business, he would take out his wallet and extract from it a faded newspaper article. The headline: 'Gene Autry Almost Hurt in Explosion!' 'Humility,' Dad would say softly, 'Humility.'"

➳   ➴

Sheila's love for Pat couldn't have been more obvious. That she remained by his side throughout this horrible ordeal was all the assurance he needed. They were married on December 26, 1951, in Las Vegas.

Many people were quite surprised at this turn of events. They didn't think such a marriage would last. As Gene Autry described the pair, "She was pretty and independent. He was country and funloving." Would the marriage work? Sheila could have married almost anyone she wanted. Why Pat? When you look at the whole picture, though, it's not hard to understand her feelings. A gorgeous woman, who has such a wide variety of men from which to choose, quickly learns that dashing good looks mean nothing. What matters is what's inside. Pat was a good man who loved her very much, a generous man who took great pleasure in making her happy, an intelligent man who used his talent to bring sunshine to others. His beauty was in his very soul. Too, Pat's future looked quite promising—he was a brilliant humorist who was his generation's Will Rogers.

And besides, doggone it, she loved him.

➳   ➴

In the first episode filmed of the second *Gene Autry Show* season, Pat was back at work. This episode was entitled "Horse Sense." He was so happy to be back in the saddle; his joyful smile and relaxed stance couldn't be stifled. The running gag in this episode is that Pat's horse ran too slowly (being unable to keep up with Gene's Champion) and stopped too quickly (causing Pat to fall off). His was still a very physical role, but he could handle it. He was now enjoying good health again. The muscles in his stomach region, however, had been severed in the accident, which resulted in a rounded tummy from then on.

The next episode filmed was "Outlaw Escape." Pat was the sheriff in this one. While Gene was doing all the serious business, the hapless sheriff was nursing saddle sores. He would still ride, but he kept a pillow between himself and his horse.

You can tell that Autry was awfully glad to have his old sidekick back. In the show's closing credits, "Pat Buttram" was in very large letters at the very top of the cast list. The rest of the cast's names were written in normal-size letters.

Sheila appeared a few more times in Autry productions. One in particular, she joked, was a "dream job" for her. In this episode, "Border Justice," her character threw an overripe tomato, then a half-cooked omelet into Pat's face, followed by a scene in which she upset a wash bucket full of soapy water on him. She, too, had a keen sense of humor.

Stuntman Whitey Hughes recalls a Screen Actors Guild party in which family members were invited. Because the parking attendant was busy, he had dropped his wife and daughter off, then went to park the car. The ladies then went inside and over to the elevator. Pat had never seen Whitey's family before but, as soon as they stepped onto the elevator, he declared, "You have *got* to be Whitey Hughes' daughter!" When they later told Hughes about that, he was touched. "That's how much he noticed and thought of people," he says. "Pat always—I don't care how long it was between scenes or when he'd last seen you—Pat was the kind of guy that never forgot you. That means a lot to me."

Everyone seems to have deep admiration for Pat. "Everybody I've seen him around he made very, very happy," says Bill Hale.

The Autry entourage was off on another tour. When they arrived in Austin, Minnesota, the first one off the bus was Pat. "He had two suitcases and something slung over his shoulder," says singer/composer Johnny Western, who was sixteen at the time and scheduled to interview Gene for the KDHL radio station. Johnny gave Pat a helping hand with his load. Once everyone got settled in, he was able to proceed with the interview.

"Pat was there for about half the interview," he says, "and he actually had me stop the recording and redo a little bit of it with Gene because Gene had slurred a couple of the words that he didn't think should go out on the air. I had asked Gene what kind of a horse Champion was, and he said, 'Well, he's half Tennessee Walker and half Morgan.' When he said "Walker," it came out sounding like "Worker." Pat had picked up on that and he said, 'Why don't you erase that part and do it over again? Just do those couple of lines over again. I think it would sound better.' So I did and Gene did." Pat's extensive radio experience had made him quite professional in that regard. He wanted his interview to be the best it could be and his radio experience came in very handy. Even though Pat's image was that of a country boy, he had learned to enunciate clearly so the listeners would understand every word.

Pat's protectiveness toward Gene and their cohorts got a real workout once. Says Johnny Western, who later toured with the Autry company, "They'd been in Milwaukee, Wisconsin and they had a matinee and a night show to do." The troupe had been on the road for quite some time, and almost everyone but Pat was ailing. "The matinee was packed with kids—parents usually came to the night show. They [the performers] still had to get through two shows that day. The place was sold out for both shows. The events went like this: Carl Cottner was Gene's music director and he was a wonderful fiddle player, did a great thing with 'Listen to the Mockingbird' with sound effects. It was a most enjoyable act. Carl came up to do his part of the show and very first thing was 'Listen to the Mockingbird.' He was so loaded that his fiddle bow shot clear across the stage. He was just standing there with a fiddle in his left hand and a dumbfounded look on his face. So Pat went out and made a whole skit out of going to retrieve Carl's fiddle bow. He told the kids in the audience that Carl used to be a world champion archer and he thought he was still practicing with the bow and arrow. Of course, the kids bought it because that's what it looked like—it just shot right out of his hand. The kids laughed. Merle Travis, who had written 'Sixteen Tons,' was on the show. Travis, ordinarily a marvelous guitar player and singer and songwriter, just couldn't find that guitar with both hands. In fact, he was starting to fall. Pat went out and put his arm around him, virtually holding him up and saying funny things, while Travis was playing and doing the couple of songs on the show." Johnny Bond and the Cass County Boys were fine, but they were standing behind everyone else, doing backup, so they couldn't come forward to help the others. "It came time to bring Gene on. Well, Gene was not in good shape and Pat knew they weren't going to make it through, so when Gene got out there, Pat walked back out there again and draped his arm around Gene's shoulder, got on the microphone and said, 'Boys and girls, Gene picked up a heckuva cold. We were in Minneapolis, Minnesota last night. Cold up there! He just picked up a heckuva cold, so he really needs your help. Let's just all sing along with Gene. You know all the words to the song.' They sang 'Rudolph,' 'Peter Cottontail,' all the kids songs, and of course he had to do 'Back in the Saddle Again,' which every kid in the world knew. So Pat stood there with him, holding him up and keeping him away from the microphone because he was not going to be good in the singing department. And they got through the matinee. The horse could practically do the act by himself. All Gene had to do was hang on. The horse trainer, Jay Berry, was running the horse through his paces, and they got through it. Then they went back to the hotel, trying to get ready for the night show. Well, the phone rang at the hotel. It was the manager of the Milwaukee municipal auditorium… He said, 'You've got to do something about the night show. You've got to change the night show. That Pat Buttram is out there hogging the microphone every chance he gets and ruining the whole show!'" The cover-up had been successful. Even the manager didn't realize what had happened.

"There would've been no show without Buttram…That was vintage Pat Buttram," Western says. "He just went out there and did it. He was just so showbiz-minded. He knew the ship was sinking and he had to do something."

The fourteen-page souvenir program that was distributed while on tour had a full-page write-up about Pat and included two photos. It indicated that Pat wasn't nearly as old or as backward as his character. "Born with the dignified name of Maxwell Emmett Buttram in Winston County, Alabama, just 36 years ago, Pat, as he is better known, is college bred, soft spoken and serious-minded, utterly different from the irascible, lovable rustic he portrays," it says. "A notable fact about Pat's portrayal of these so-called hill-billies," it adds, "is that the fun he pokes at them is never sharply pointed, but always kindly. He has a healthy respect for rural folks, and appreciates their philosophy of life."

Indeed, Pat had very tender, loving feelings about the folks back home.

When Pat was visiting his dad's house, neighborhood children would often gather on the porch to see him. He would be glad to oblige them, coming out and telling them jokes. When visiting his eldest brother Johnny for four or five days, he would help make PR visits for his radio station. Johnny's son John recalls Pat's helping out at a Cub Scout mini jamboree, in which the scouts were acting out a scene as knights on horseback with wooden swords. Well, it seems those boys got a bit carried away as they went after Pat. "He was black and blue," John laughs. Pat's brothers and sisters considered Johnny the funniest member of the clan, and he would sometimes have Pat on his knees laughing.

Pat's parents, because of the nature of Rev. Buttram's work, were still pulling up stakes frequently. In February of 1952, they were living in Anniston and serving at the White Plains Methodist Church and Buttram's Chapel, which was named after their beloved minister. So to Anniston Pat went to spend the weekend with them before heading back to Hollywood for another movie. He had just finished the Autry troupe's latest national tour and was ready for a mini-vacation. As usual, it had been a busy time with about two shows a day and visits to hospitals and orphanages. In addition to tour work, he was also contracted to appear in fifty-two television shows, fifty-two radio broadcasts, and six films a year. He was a very tired man.

Alabama's newspapers seemed to enjoy calling him the state's "Most Famed Hillbilly" because of his folksy style. When he arrived in Alabama, he was met at the airport by his father and other family members. "When I went up to see him," says niece Mary, "he emptied all the change out of his pocket and gave it to me. I was so excited. There is a picture, taken at the Birmingham Airport, of Uncle Pat and my granddaddy, Daddy Mack, that was in the *Birmingham News*. The excitement and pride on Daddy Mack's face tells how we all felt about Uncle Pat."

What would they do during that visit? "My aunts, Peggy, Mamie and Hallie, are and were such good cooks and so creative," Mary says. "Uncle Pat has been known to go to the woods with Hallie and gather material for arrangements. He loved his family and especially his sisters. He was proud of them and their creativity." When Pat had seen a vegetable dicer/slicer advertised on television, he bought one for his sister.

In an article by Gertrude Tyson that appeared on Monday, February 25, 1952, in *The Anniston Star*, it was said that Pat and Sheila had bought a new home in Hollywood that included a swimming pool and tennis court. One of his most prized possessions, it stated, was his reading lamp that he had decorated himself with Confederate bills. "He bought a supply of the outmoded currency during his current Southern tour, and mailed one of the $1 bills to his friend Hedda Hopper, with the following explanation: 'They're selling these at $1.50 each down here now...It's like I've been telling you, Hedda, the South won that war!'"

While Pat was still working with Gene on the television series and on the road, he was less enamored with the movies. His final Autry film, *Blue Canadian Rockies*, had been filmed in 1952. Smiley Burnette then stepped back into his old sidekick role, happy to be reunited with the troupe in film.

Pat found himself and Sheila in London in 1953, with the Autry entourage. He wrote from this faraway city to Nate Gross, and it was quoted under the title "Innocents Abroad": "They gave me a nice reception here, but I still think they'd rather have Ronald Colman back. There are some interesting sights to see—most of them are tourists."

When they had returned stateside, they were passing through Alabama on their way back to California. Pat took that opportunity to show his bride his old stomping grounds. They stayed with his eldest sister, Peggy Mauldin. "I remember how excited everyone was for Uncle Pat to be home," says Mary. "He had been interviewed by one of the local radio stations and we all sat around listening to the radio interview."

During that visit with the family, Pat had played a joke on Sheila. Earlier, he had bought a really tacky brooch. "It was awful looking," remembers Hallie with a laugh. He then told Sheila that it was a family heirloom, so, not wanting to hurt the family's feelings, she wore it while in Alabama. What a relief it was to learn the truth, so she wouldn't have to wear that thing anymore!

Early 1954, the Autry company was off again. This tour would stop in fifty cities, beginning in Duluth and ending in Birmingham on February 28. The Buttram family in Alabama could count on seeing him again after the Birmingham engagement was completed.

Later that year, WABT in Birmingham held a Pat Buttram lookalike contest for the kids. The five boys who looked and acted most like Pat would appear on that local station.

Working as Gene Autry's comic relief was a wonderful job, but it did have its inconveniences. When the two were shown riding their horses together, Gene got the fine horse and smooth path while Pat got "a fugitive from a glue factory—and I get the rocky side of the trail. But I have to keep up." The star got the beautiful horse named Champion. Pat had a mule named Dandruff. Maybe there's not equality in such things, but it certainly makes for fine humor.

Actually, Pat had had a horse in Autry movies, too. His name was Joker. His character also had a pet rooster named Lover Boy.

Autry wrote a tribute to his sidekick that ran in a September 12, 1954 newspaper. Entitled "Alabama's Pat Buttram has tough role on TV but makes folks laugh," it described Pat's character and what made him so perfect for the role: "Pat stands around five feet 10 inches and weighs never a pound under 250. So that our audiences may be instantly aware of what he's doing we see to it that Pat amply embellishes his own natural attributes for the part. In addition to his comic proportions he sports the scraggliest beaver this side of Haile Selassie, a checked shirt which might kindly be called sloppy, a pair of old khaki pants which have never been bruised by a tailor's iron and a shapeless mass of felt which, because of its position on his person, must pass as a hat."

Later in the article, Gene described a typical day's work: "I'm not sure Pat knew what he was getting into when he came to work for me. In just one of our recent films he had to fall into a watering trough filled with icy water; he was slapped in the face with a pan of rising dough; he had to fall off a horse; be conked on the head with an iron skillet, and sit unconcernedly while an Indian shot an arrow through the top of his hat!" It usually wasn't stuntmen doing these feats, either.

Gene flew his own plane, a silver and white twin-engine craft, on these tours. Pat was welcome to join him in the plane, but he sometimes opted to follow on a bus with the rest of the crew so he'd be able to stop to see his family in Alabama. He loved going home, even if it was only for a few hours.

"My father lived in Addison, Alabama," says Hallie, "and one time they [Gene and company] were up in Tennessee, I think, and some of those country singers who were with Gene were driving south and they were going through Addison, so Pat said, 'Let me go with y'all and we'll stop to see my daddy.' So, as Gene was flying over Addison, he called the radio station and he said, 'Would you get in touch with Rev. Buttram and tell him Pat's on his way?' It was 2:00 or 3:00 in the morning when Pat came with the boys, and they had food for them. Just a short thing like that, but then he would visit Dad every chance he got. He loved his dad."

Father and son enjoyed a good laugh together now and then. Once, they were at a convenience store, but in different aisles. Pat yelled over to his most-reverend-dad, "What kind of beer did you say you wanted?" Thank goodness for the senior Buttram's sense of humor. He thought that was hilarious.

It was during his Autry days that Pat and Ralph Edwards became friends. Says Sue Clark Chadwick, "I have been Mr. Edwards' Public Relations consultant since 1947, and also knew Pat very well.

"Ralph and Pat met during the glory days of radio when Pat was doing the Gene Autry movies and radio show, but became good friends with the founding of the Pacific Pioneer Broadcasters, a group of radio and TV veterans. Both were charter members. Ralph was on the board and Pat was the in-house humorist. There was always a great deal of banter between the two of them at Board meetings and the five-times-a-year luncheons. Pat also accompanied Ralph and his group to Fiestas in Truth or Consequences, New Mexico, where he was a hit with the townspeople and all who met him."

One of the Autry tours took them to Chicago, and Pat took this opportunity to drop in on his old friends at WLS. A photo resulted in the *1954 WLS Family Album*. It showed Pat surrounded by two gentlemen and a lady, who were all laughing. The caption says, "Alumnus Pat Buttram returned last September to 'crack wise' as in days of yore with his feuding partner, Jack Holden. Jimmy James, Grace Wilson and Uncle Otto are probably laughing at one of Pat's stories about his summer trip to England with Gene Autry's Rodeo. He is now Gene's comedian in western pictures and on network radio."

Another stop was a county fair in DuQuoin, Illinois. An act there fascinated Pat. It was called "Colonel Tom Parker and His Dancing Turkeys" and Parker also served as his own barker. (This was the same man who would soon catapult Elvis Presley to worldwide fame.) Pat went inside to see the spectacle. Sure enough, it appeared that the turkeys were dancing. Upon closer inspection and talking with Parker, he learned that beneath the sawdust "floor" the turkeys stood on was a metal plate. It was rigged up to generate heat, as much as was needed to get the turkeys to appear to dance to whatever music the Colonel was playing at the time. Pat loved animals, but he also loved ingenuity. He would remember this man and his act, and later in life pattern one of his most beloved characters after him.

Chapter Seven

In March 1954, Sheila gave birth to a baby girl. They named her Kathleen Kerry Buttram, and she would someday be the very image of her beautiful mother.

On little Kerry's birth certificate, Pat signed his name "Maxwell Patrick Buttram." This, she says, was done to leave the press no doubt who her father was. Too, he had been forced to disengage himself from adopted daughter Gayle when his first marriage failed, so he was probably making sure such a thing would never happen again.

"According to Mom," says Kerry, "when I was a baby, Dad was afraid to hold me because I was so small and he thought himself clumsy. He was afraid he'd drop me or I would break or cry or something. I'm sure that wore off quickly, as we were a very huggy family."

Once he got over his initial trepidation, Pat was very much an active father. Articles from this era show the couple with their toddler daughter and, in many of the photos, it's Pat who was holding her.

Having a child gave him another little lady to love. Pat got great pleasure from giving Sheila and Kerry gifts—fun toys for Kerry and beautiful adornments for Sheila. "I believe he thought of her as a queen and so he gave her queenly things," Kerry says.

Having been raised in poverty, Pat now enjoyed to the fullest his ability to give his loved ones whatever they needed or wanted.

❧   ❧

George Gobel, a friend from his WLS days, had really come up in the world, too. Not only did he have his own television show now, but it was the highest-ranking half-hour show of the 1954-55 season. It was during an appearance on this show that Pat met its creator-writer-producer, Hal Kanter. Like Pat, Hal had a sparkling wit and a great love of family. The two men hit it off instantly and would be close friends for the rest of Pat's life.

"I thought he was one of the most amusing men I have ever known," says Kanter. "I was first struck by Pat when he came onstage wearing a green suit, with shirt, tie, socks and shoes all the same color, and his first words to his audience were, 'If you see anything green, go ahead and laugh.' And they sure did! He was funny and clean."

Usually, his humor was clean. Hal acknowledged the fact that Pat could fit in with the guys at a stag event. The angel in him would sit it out during such an occasion as his mischievous inner imp would take over, the result being "obscenely hilarious."

"He could play to any kind of an audience," says Johnny Western. "The two most in-demand after-dinner speakers in all of Hollywood for a great many years for all the big doings were Art Linkletter and Pat Buttram."

They could always count on Pat to give a speech that was tailor-made for his audience. "His mind for comedy was very, very sharp. Categorically, that took him out of the realm of 'hick comedian.' He was much, much more than that."

≫   ≪

Christmas Eve of 1955 was the final broadcast of *The Gene Autry Show* television series. It had had a successful five seasons.

Johnny Western recalls something Pat said back then: "Someday somebody may make more movies than Gene Autry; someday somebody may make more television shows than Gene Autry; someday somebody may sell more records than Gene Autry; someday somebody may make more personal appearances than Gene Autry. (Then there was a long, pregnant pause.) But they're going to lose a helluva lot of sleep doing it."

On January 12, 1956, a roast honoring Dale Evans and Roy Rogers was held at the Masquers Club in Hollywood. Among those participating were WLS alumnus Gene Autry and George Gobel. Pat was host of the event. Evans and Rogers, Pat declared, were the "Lunt and Fontaine of the fertilizer set."

Harriet, daughter of his sister Hallie, enjoyed seeing Pat when he visited the Chicago area. "I was a junior in high school. We got to go to the rodeo with Uncle Pat and sat in Rex Allen's box," she says. "Uncle Pat must have been making appearances there because he stayed at our house for a week or so."

The tours were soon to come to an end. After a seventeen-year run, Gene Autry's radio show finale aired on May 13, 1956. Autry had already retired from radio earlier that week, so Pat did a fine job putting this tribute show together in his place and hosting it. He led the cast in a heartfelt "adios" to their good friend, wishing him all the best in the future.

Mr. Wrigley, the show's sponsor, was so touched by this fine send-off that he immediately signed Pat to a four-year contract. How odd that was, Gene thought, that the very sponsor who cancelled his show gave Pat one of his own. Such is the unpredictable world of showbiz. Pat's new show was called *Just Entertainment*. This was a fifteen-minute variety show that he emceed on KNX-CBS in Hollywood, and it had 250 subscribing stations. They were treated to a song or two by Paula Richards and the Jack Halloran Quartet, and folksy storytelling by Pat, beginning at 2:45 p.m., eastern time. This show was included in the *TV-Radio Annual* of 1957, and featured in *TV-Radio Life* and *TV-Radio Mirror* magazines that same year. Sales of Doublemint Gum must surely have increased during that time.

After two years, *Just Entertainment* was still going strong. In an August 9, 1958, *TV Life* article, "Rocking Chair Comic," Pat explains, "There are the so-called stand-up comics, and the pantomime of sight comics. There are the situation comedians who depend on skits and black-outs. In fact, there are a dozen different types of comedy—but I figure I'm sort of a rocking chair comedian. In fact, if it weren't for the fact that we use upright microphones in Studio B at Columbia Square and producer Ed Simmons kinda likes to see his cast from the control booth, I'd probably bring down a rocker and do my show sittin' down."

In another article, "Cracker Barrel Philosophy" by Charles Stalnaker, Pat credits his father for his wit. "He was great for cracker barrel philosophy," he said. "I can still remember one bit of advice he gave me when I was beginning to make good money and was looking around for an investment or two. My father told me to 'invest in land, because that is something they ain't making any more of.' This is sound advice, you will have to admit."

Now that *The Gene Autry Show* was off the air, Pat was finally able to shave that beard off. The mustache stayed, however, only now it was more neatly trimmed.

The great Robert Benchley had earlier urged Pat, "Don't let them label you a comedian. You are something deeper than that. You are a humorist." Feeling much admiration for Benchley, Pat would remember those words forever.

Thanks to Gene, Pat was accustomed to working in several venues at once, so he also turned his attention to nightclub work. A picture postcard that was produced during this era to encourage tourism in Las Vegas shows the Bonanza Hotel, located on the Strip, with Sarah Vaughan and Pat Buttram as its headliners.

B-westerns were dying and being replaced by Westerns with much larger budgets, on the big and small screens. The wholesome themes of the Autry shows were to be seen no more.

⇒   ⇐

By 1957, Pat's father had been pastoring at Carpenter Memorial Methodist Church before going into semi-retirement, and brother Gus was the minister of Weaver Methodist Church. Pat's brother Johnny managed a radio station in Roanoke. Too much time had passed since he had visited the folks back home, so off to Alabama Pat went. While there, he put on a few benefit shows to raise funds for his dad's pet church projects.

The *Anniston Star* reported a show Pat gave at the Constantine Homes and Glen Addie recreation center especially for children. The delighted boys and girls were entertained with stories and open forums in which he described what it's like to make western movies.

Back in California, Pat's little family had made their ranch-style Van Nuys home uniquely their own. The home was furnished in the Early American period. Pat's study, in which his Civil War relics could be seen everywhere, was his favorite room. The October issue of *TV-Radio Mirror* showed doting parents romping with three-year-old Kerry at their home.

⇒   ⇐

Pat was one of the most-quoted people in the business. *Readers' Digest* resented its readers with Mike Connolly's favorite Pat Buttram quote: "This isn't a recession—it's just that we had a boom and somebody lowered it."

Hy Gardner's column had another Buttram zinger. On the topic of the Elizabeth Taylor—Richard Burton wedding, he said that Pat couldn't figure out who would be invited. "They've already married all their friends!"

❧   ❧

On April 26, 1958, Pat was the special guest celebrity at the Choccolocco Council Scout Circus at Etowah Stadium in Attalla, Alabama. He rode in the parades on horseback in Gadsden and Attalla in the afternoon and took part in the program that evening, delighting one and all.

"We were going to go to my Uncle Johnny's in Gadsden," says Mac. "If I recall correctly, Uncle Pat was going to do some sort of show there. I bragged to my classmates about my uncle and told them that I would bring back autographs for each one of them. However, when I was finally with Uncle Pat, I was too afraid to ask him, so I went back to school the next day and was not too popular."

TV Guide ran a two-page article about *The Pat Buttram Show*, which aired Monday through Friday from 11:45 p.m. to 12:15 a.m. This show was unique. It had a feature in which a guest would put two pennies into a piggy bank, then he would be given two minutes to sound off on his pet peeve. Three guests were on hand each night to give their two cents' worth. "The rest of the half hour is devoted to Buttram's own genial humor," says the article, "and that's enough to make the whole charade a success."

It was around this time that his path again crossed that of actress Donna Martell. By now, she had two sons who were in the same preschool that Kerry attended. Donna and Pat would see each other sometimes as they picked up their children after school. It was always a treat to see an old friend again.

Saturday, March 28, 1959, was a big day for the folks back home. That was the day of the big benefit show that raised funds for the Aid for Retarded Children. Pat was the show's headliner, Benny Carle emceed, and the audience was also entertained by the Mortimer Jordan High School Band, the gospel-singing quartet from the University of Alabama "The Calvaleers," a male quartet called "The Flickers," the female "Professionalettes," Happy Hal Burns, comedian Dave Gardner, comedy/tap duo Butch and Dale Serrano, magician Cliff Holman, Country Boy Eddie, Charlie Duke and His Dixieland Band, and Bob Harmon and His Band. Anticipatory articles ran in the local newspaper prior to the gala weekend. Admission to the show was a dollar, and every bit of the monies collected would go to the charity.

When Pat got off the plane in Birmingham, he was greeted by his father, sister Peggy, niece Zella and nephew John. With them was the president of the Aid for Retarded Children, the show's general chairman, a representative of the Chamber of Commerce, and Benny Carle, on whose WBRC-TV show Pat's Autry movies were shown.

The Aid for Retarded Children received a sizable wad of money, and Pat got the heartwarming satisfaction of a job well done.

While there for the event, Pat made guest appearances on Happy Hal Burns' *Circle 6 Ranch* show on WAPI-TV and the Wally Fowler Gospel singing show on WBRC-TV.

➤   ◄

Whenever Pat was in Alabama, he would treat his nieces and nephews really well, bringing them presents. "He was a good uncle," says John, who enjoyed being the one to pick Pat up at the Birmingham airport, now that he had his driver's license. John cherished the talks they'd have during those rides.

Pat cared very much for his fans, but he did enforce boundaries. If he were alone, he'd be very happy to sign autographs to his fans' content. If, however, he was dining with his siblings, nieces, nephews, or Alabama friends, it was a different story. He had so little time to spend with these loved ones that he resisted anything that would detract from it. Thus, requests for autographs were rejected at those times.

➤   ◄

The first movie Pat made with Elvis Presley was *Wild in the Country*, which was released in 1961. The female stars were Tuesday Weld and Hope Lange, and Pat played the mechanic who was a big part of Elvis' character's life. The superstar's acting was at its best in this film, and Pat was quite impressed with this very courteous, generous young man.

Sheila's mother was a member of the Motion Picture Mothers, Inc. organization, and they would ask Pat often to emcee their events during the 1960s. He was happy to comply.

Pat was very much in demand as an emcee, and he presided over the women's press luncheons of this era, as well. It was at such an event that he first met the beloved Walt Disney. Seeing him there, Pat made joke after joke about Disneyland and its creator. "Disney really laughed at my jokes," he said happily to *The Tampa Tribune* reporter Greg Tozian.

Pat was approached about the future television series *The Beverly Hillbillies*. Since all the other shows being aired then were much more sophisticated, he didn't think this one would be very successful. Trying to be helpful, though, he suggested they get his friend Buddy Ebsen to play the lead and include the Flatt and Scruggs team. They did, and history was made. Oh, and the term "cement pond," which was given so much play in that show? Well, the Buttram family knows that that phrase had been used by them for years—long before *The Beverly Hillbillies*—to describe the fish pond in brother Johnny's back yard.

⇥   ⇤

Kerry was seven years old now and was delighted with all the kittens. The family had three female cats and they had all given birth to kittens around the same time. Then one of the mother cats died. "Unexpectedly," says Kerry, "Dad took charge of the situation and showed me how to heat the milk and how much Karo syrup to put in it. Then we put the milk in little baby doll bottles and fed the kittens. He must have learned it during his childhood. It was cute watching this bear of a man hand-feeding a tiny kitten."

At one point, one of the family pets was a goose. Just as Hannibal did to Yadkin in the future *Daniel Boone* television series, this goose chased Kerry all over the place. Was he being hostile or amorous? Doesn't matter. "It scared the heck out of me," she says. "My dad's choice of pets tended to go awry like that."

Indeed, Pat loved animals. Once, he brought home a big, beautiful parrot. Kerry recalls, "Mom wasn't altogether pleased. The parrot wasn't altogether pleased. I was fascinated, but a little scared. Dad was full of enthusiasm, as usual. He wanted to take a picture of me with the parrot on my shoulder. He put the bird on my right shoulder and all was well for about thirty seconds. But it was a big bird and I had a small shoulder. As Dad was trying to focus the camera, the bird began to slip. Desperate for whatever purchase he could get, the parrot grasped my ear with his beak. Pandemonium! Blood everywhere. Me screaming. Mom screaming. The parrot screaming. I think Dad dropped the camera when he rushed over to take the bird off my shoulder and put it back in its cage.

Within five minutes, my poor, deflated dad was driving the bird back to the pet store."

That idea hadn't worked, but professionally it seemed Pat could do no wrong. He was the featured humorist in the April 1, 1962 *Parade* national supplement to the Sunday newspaper. Three of the anecdotes he chose for this "My Favorite Jokes" article are as follows:

In most of our Hollywood beauty shops the gossip alone would curl your hair!

Medical science has long said that alcohol cannot cure the common cold—but then, neither can medical science.

Remember, when your boy goes to summer camp, you are not losing a son but gaining two frogs, a turtle, a garter snake, and a field mouse.

During the summer of 1962, Pat was talking with his friend Arthur Godfrey. CBS had promised him some specials, Godfrey said, but no one had come up with any ideas as to content yet. Why not do a show about behind-the-scenes things in Hollywood, Pat suggested. The result was broadcast in November - a sixty-minute special called *Arthur Godfrey in Hollywood*. People behind some of the most familiar voices would be introduced, along with instructions on how singers lip sync and other goodies the average viewer isn't normally privy to. Pat was included in the line-up as well, and it was listed as the "Best Bet" of the week's television offerings in the November 10 *St. Petersburg Times*.

"For years I thought I knew all there was to know about this show business…then I met Pat Buttram," Godfrey said. "He has helped me immensely. A great writer and performer."

Jack Benny felt the same way. After coming onstage right after Pat one night, he said, "I've been praised for my timing, but Pat Buttram makes me sound like Jack Warner." Benny was a courageous man. Very few comedians would follow Buttram's act.

It was in this year that Pat worked again with his buddy Hal Kanter, this time on a record album. Entitled *Off His Rocker*, it was recorded before a live audience and consisted of Milt Josefsberg and Hal Kanter's jokes being told by Pat. The two writers were also its producers. The topics covered in this lighthearted disk include etiquette, fairy tales, toys, and teenagers.

It wouldn't be long before Pat would have a teenager at home who might then have given him enough material to write his own monolog.

Pat was now considered Hollywood's favorite after-dinner speaker. "Combining a sophisticated, pointed sense of humor with a genuine country-boy charm, Buttram is the natural successor to such homespun humorists as Bob Burns, Irvin S. Cobb and Will Rogers," says a document offered by the Motion Picture & Television Fund.

He enjoyed spending time with his friends at the Sportsman's Lodge in Studio City and was often seen there with Gene Autry and Monte Hale. "I walked into the Sportsman's one day for lunch," says actor Robert Fuller, "and there was Pat and Gene. They had a private booth in the back. Pat motioned for me to come over and sit down and said, 'Bob, I'd like you to meet Gene.' I sat down and had lunch with those guys. It was a thrill for me." Even though Fuller had been in the business since 1952, this was the first time he had met Autry. "Monte, Pat, and Gene were the Three Musketeers in those days. We had a lot of fun."

Pat was a guest speaker once and cracked a joke about his good friend Phil Harris. Harris' reputation was that of a heavy drinker. Whether or not this was true, speakers and reporters always enjoyed expounding on that image. Pat did, too. Following one of Los Angeles' earthquakes, he said, "The quake was so violent, Phil Harris was thrown to his feet." The audience roared.

"He was at a lot of functions," says friend George Lindsey of Pat. "He was the master of ceremonies. He was *the* Toastmaster of Hollywood. We went up to Reno to see him." Lindsey, who did stand-up comedy himself, asked Pat to write some jokes for him, and he was pleased to do so.

There have been a few times that Pat arrived at a dinner, only to discover that the audience wasn't who he thought it would be. Once, for instance, he thought he'd be speaking to the Days Inn management, but found out the audience was filled with tourists instead. No problem! He had an incredible memory that contained thousands of jokes and a quick wit that enabled him to come up with some of his own. Typically, Pat would begin his speech with three jokes, then monitor the audience's response. Whichever one they liked the most would be the theme of the next three jokes. He'd continue in that manner until he had been speaking for about forty-five minutes. This method made him a big hit.

Ron Smith, in his book *Comic Support*, commented on Pat's "crackling, yodeling voice." That very unique voice made him instantly recognizable to audiences everywhere. He did have control over his voice, however, and was able to speak more smoothly during his dramatic roles.

In January of the following year, Pat was asked to speak at the Masquers Club during an event to honor Harold Lloyd. Hedda Hopper was in the audience, and she was thoroughly impressed. She had known him before, but this was apparently the first time she had seen him perform. "I keep appearing at these big Hollywood dinners," Pat had said, "because they say some night some energetic, brilliant, important producer will see me and I'll be discovered. But as I look around the room tonight I see I've blown another evening." As Hopper reported in her January 25 column, "I ain't no producer, but as far as I'm concerned, Pat is now discovered. I can sit stone-faced while our greatest comedians deliver their high-priced gags, but Buttram killed me." Continued Pat, "Some feller told me the best way to get big in Hollywood is to speak at these Masquers dinners. The guy that told me that is real smart. He's the same feller that told Eddie Fisher to sit tight [regarding the Taylor–Burton affair] till it blows over."

Hedda Hopper just couldn't stop. She quoted a few more of his jokes:

Re Mary Pickford: "One of the most naïve women in the world— until you try to buy a piece of her real estate."

Re Hollywood: "I am proud to say that Hollywood has a heart. In Hollywood if you need sympathy, love, affection, money or friendship, all you have to do is look in the yellow pages under pool halls."

Hopper hoped that her column would provide the big break he needed. "He's my top comic from now on," she declared.

The Hollywood Reporter seemed to like him, too. It stated, "Sending somebody to follow the very funny Pat Buttram at the Masquers salute to Harold Lloyd was as cruel as evicting your grandmother from her iron lung."

Pat's natural humor kept his friends and co-stars in stitches, as well. Actor Wright King laughingly recalls what Pat told him on King's fortieth birthday—that now he had better buy a black suit because, at such an advanced age, he'd be attending many funerals from then on.

⇥   ⇤

Speaking of age, Pat's father was getting up in years. He had had kidney problems and a series of small strokes. Once he was unable to drive a car, he got around in a cart pulled by a mule. Mack's health eventually deteriorated enough that he needed more care. At first, the family had placed him in a nursing home. This placement did not meet his needs, however, so Gus and his wife Becky then moved him to their own home. There, he was given loving care. Still, it seemed that nothing could really be done to restore his health, and Mack died on March 12, 1963.

How his family would miss him. There's not much that he enjoyed more than a good joke. His sons had provided him with many laughs, and his family had given him much joy.

Pat bought a weathervane, to be placed atop the John Ford Chapel in memory of his father. "It is a constant reminder of the loving concern he felt for the Motion Picture and Television Fund," says a document of the organization.

➤   ◄

Even though Pat and Gene Autry were no longer working together, they were still buddies. Gene was scheduled to appear on *The Ed Sullivan Show* but, for some reason, couldn't make it. Pat was glad to fill in for him. Not only was this quite a successful performance, but it again put him on the same coast as his sister Hallie. The military had sent her and her husband to New Jersey, so he visited her there.

According to AP writer Bob Thomas in his April 10, 1963 article, "Comic Finds Remaining at Top Is Hard Work," it was the Masquers dinner that made Pat's career really take off. "Now the offers are hot and heavy," Thomas reported. "He has signed with MGM for two pictures a year, the first being with Richard Chamberlain in 'Twilight of Honor.'" Thomas' article continues, "Ed Sullivan snapped him up for eight appearances in a year. Revenue wants him to narrate a television series using the Universal newsreel library. Don Quinn wants him to tour in a play based on the life of Will Rogers."

The following month, there was Pat on TV again—on an episode of *The Real McCoys*—and, according to Hedda Hopper's July 23 column, "Danny Thomas is having a special episode written around Pat for his fall TV show." This episode was broadcast in October; *Twilight of Honor* was released in December.

Arthur Godfrey had more praise for him. He told *TV Guide,* "Within that huge and overstuffed frame lies some of the greatest creative comedy genius our profession has ever known."

Radio station KNX also had him working for them each day on a show called *Story-Line.* Here, Pat was on a panel that discussed a wide range of topics and interviewed people relative to the subjects of interest. No one could humorously expound on current events better than he.

Yessir, Pat Buttram was hot.

Chapter Eight

***Twilight of Honor* had been released** amidst much fanfare. Besides Richard Chamberlain and Pat, it also starred Nick Adams, Claude Rains, Joan Blackman, and James Gregory, as well as newcomer Joey Heatherton. This wasn't Pat's usual comedic role, however. Rather, this was a murder mystery/courtroom film in which he had a straight dramatic role as the murder victim, Cole Clinton. The story begins with Chamberlain's character, David Mitchell, being appointed to defend Ben Brown, played by Nick Adams. While the victim was known around town as a highly-respected police official, the witnesses' testimony of the events leading up to the murder, in which the scenes are shown to the movie-goer, reveal Clinton to be less than honorable. He was having an affair with Brown's promiscuous wife, Laura Mae, played by Joey Heatherton in her cinematic debut. This picture is remarkable not only for Pat's excellent dramatic performance, but also for Nick Adams' portrayal of both the gentle man described by the defense and the violent one depicted by the prosecution when both scenarios are acted out.

According to sister Hallie, Pat didn't want Kerry to see this film because of the sexual misconduct of his character.

Was switching from comedy to drama difficult for him?

"I liked doing it," Pat told Emmett Weaver, the *Birmingham Post-Herald* entertainment editor. "It was easier than I thought it would be. I didn't have to scratch myself even once."

Many who have tried both have said that serious acting is easier than comedy. Pat agreed. "A fellow can learn serious acting from a coach, but the only way to learn to be a comedian is by facing an audience. That's the best way to learn timing, and I think that's as important—maybe even more important—as having good material."

Pat appeared the next year in another somber film. At the beginning of the TV movie, *The Hanged Man*, Pat's character has a conversation with star Robert Culp's character, as he shows him the body of the deceased and discusses the car bombing that ended his life. It was this murder that was the basis for the rest of the story.

Then Pat again had serious roles on two 1964 episodes of the *Alfred Hitchcock Hour*. Doing such a sinister show was not his idea, however. It was Hitchcock who convinced him to give it a try after being urged by the story's writer, Ray Bradbury, to get Pat for the lead. This was the story of a small-town man, named Charlie Hill, who buys a mysterious jar from a carnival in order to impress the people in his community. Night after night, neighbors would come in to gaze at it and try to figure out what the jar's contents were. Everyone saw something different in it, and it stimulated much discussion. Everyone admired Charlie and his jar. His young wife, Thedy, hates it, though, and finally gets to the point that she just has to get rid of it. She opens the jar and pulls all the contents out, revealing that it was nothing but junk. She declares that she will tell everyone so they'll know what a fake he is. The fight turns physical. The next night, the neighbors are horrified to discover what is now in the jar—Thedy's head. Co-starring Collin Wilcox as Thedy, and also featuring Billy Barty and fellow Alabaman George Lindsey, it was entitled "The Jar," and was deemed by Alfred Hitchcock himself to be the best episode of this series. Pat's dramatic portrayal of Charlie Hill was so fine that his work was nominated for an Emmy.

"I think that was Pat's finest hour—the finest acting of his whole career," said Lindsey to a news reporter. "We had a Ray Bradbury story, a James Bridges script, direction by Norman Lloyd, and the whole thing was perfectly cast. We had Jane Darwell, James Best, William Marshall, Slim Pickens, Collin Wilcox. But Pat was the star of the thing, and he was wonderful. It's one of the all-time great *Hitchcocks*."

While filming this episode, there was a scene in which they used corks to simulate the look of quicksand. Pat was in the midst of this scene, frantically calling, "Help me, help me!" So convincing was he that a cameraman ran around and grabbed his arm, ruining the scene and necessitating a retake.

In *The Alfred Hitchcock Presents Companion*, producer/director Norman Lloyd says, "We were noted, if I may say so, for the excellence of our casting—in those days we used to bring people out from New York. But not Pat, Pat was right here…Oh, these guys were marvelous. Pat, he was so wonderful in 'The Jar' that I didn't know where the part started and he left off, or vice versa!...He was just so wonderful in it that I put him in another one with Teresa Wright."

Kerry explains her father's resources for such exceptional dramatic acting: "The saying, attributed to Edmund Gwenn on his deathbed, 'Dying is easy. Comedy is hard' is true. Comedic actors often have within them a well of sadness or darkness of some kind. Comedy allows them to escape it for a while. Drama affords an opportunity to tap into the darkness and you will see fine dramatic performances as a result." Indeed, actors as experienced as Barbara Stanwyck (who would soon work with Pat in *Roustabout*) and Claude Rains (with whom he had worked in *Twilight of Honor*) understood how difficult it was to do comedy effectively and had much respect for such actors. Because of his lack of experience with drama, Pat thought at first that he might have to prove himself to them, but soon discovered that that was unnecessary.

A 1965 edition of *Castle of Frankenstein* magazine brings its readers onto the set as Pat and Collin are seen with author Ray Bradbury in a moment of offstage gaiety. According to the photo's caption, Pat was entertaining the other two with stories of his "Gene Artery" days.

The second Hitchcock episode in which Pat appeared was "Lonely Place," in which co-star Bruce Dern gives one of his most chilling performances ever. As Pat's daughter Kerry recalls it, "Dad told me the second production was his [and Teresa Wright's] first exposure to the young Bruce Dern. Dern stayed in character between shots, fondling the knife he carried in the show and looking at Teresa speculatively. He already had that quality of controlled menace that kept him in villain work for years. Freaked Teresa out. Dad gave me to understand that Dern, a nice man to the core, apologized after the production wrapped." Pat played Teresa's husband who hires the farmhand played by Dern. Once he realizes how dangerous his new farmhand is, he's afraid to fire him. It was probably because of the frightening quality of this show that Pat and Sheila didn't want their young daughter to see it when it originally aired.

Even though Pat was in much demand on both the large and small screens, it was radio to which he was most faithful. "I think radio is going to make a big comeback," he told a UPI reporter. "At least I'm not going to turn loose of it until I'm sure it's dead. One good thing about radio, when you're out of work and go to the unemployment lines nobody recognizes you." Unemployment wasn't a problem for Pat, however. True to his beliefs, he was still working in radio five days a week.

It was while he was employed at KNX, a CBS affiliate, in Los Angeles, that Arthur Godfrey asked Pat to come out to New York to be a guest on his star-studded morning radio show in celebration of his thirty years with CBS. He accepted, and found himself among the industry's most famous stars. Joan Crawford, Jackie Gleason, Rosemary Clooney, Lowell Thomas, Richard Nixon, Pat Boone, Jack Carter, Abigail Van Buren, and Richard Hayes were among many who were there to mark the grand event. Pat guested on that show two days that week. He wasn't the sort to grab center stage for himself, but allowed the more verbose performers more air time.

Pat met another interesting person at KNX—astrologer Sydney Omarr. The two men soon became friends, and Pat was quite concerned for Omarr. He felt that his startling predictions could result in imprisonment or endangerment of his life. Indeed, the man had received threats from some of his listeners. According to the book Omarr later wrote, *Answer in the Sky... almost*, such a thought made him feel like a modern-day Nostradamus.

➢   ➣

Pat's Pearls of Wisdom

Which one will get more reconstruction—Iraq or Cher?

The savings and loan bail-out will cost every U.S. property owner $200. Can the Japanese afford that?

It's a wise person who, when swimming or angry, keeps his mouth shut.

The best way for us to get a man on the moon is to put a woman up there first.

➢   ➣

By June, Pat was working on the Elvis Presley film *Roustabout*. Produced by Hal Wallis, the cast also included Barbara Stanwyck, Sue Ane Langdon, Leif Erickson, Jack Albertson, and Dabbs Greer. And Pat was working with Billy Barty again, so soon after they had done Hitchcock's "The Jar" together. In this film, Pat played Harry Carver, a mustachioed businessman who tries to lure Elvis' character away from the downtrodden carnival that is depending on him. He is successful for a few weeks but, as soon as the singer learns that the small carnival is going down for the third time, he returns and saves it from extinction—and wins the girl, of course. As in the Hitchcock productions, this was a straight role for Pat. No longer did there seem to be anything funny about him. Rather, he was a slimy individual, whose only concern was money. This film, Pat felt, was the best one Presley had ever made. It showed the world that he was not only a popular singer, but he could also be a downright good actor—Presley's arrogant character in this film was about as opposite from his true generous nature as he could be.

It was back to light fare for Pat in the 1965 film *Sergeant DeadHead*, in which he played none other than President Lyndon B. Johnson. In order to maintain the illusion, Pat was seen only from behind; his face was never shown. Co-starring in this musical comedy was Frankie Avalon, Deborah Walley, Buster Keaton, Eve Arden, Cesar Romero, Fred Clark, Gale Gordon, Harvey Lembeck, Donna Loren, and John Ashley.

Pat's pal Hal Kanter wrote a television pilot for him, *Down Home*. Almost as soon as the show was made, ABC snatched it up. Twentieth Century-Fox worked with them to develop the series, but the network later changed its mind and cancelled its order. Sometimes, Hollywood's fickleness worked in Pat's favor, and sometimes it didn't.

That summer, brother Gus, his wife Becky, and their children, Mary and Mac, drove out west to visit Pat and Sheila. Says Mac, "We stayed with Uncle Pat, Aunt Sheila, and Kerry about a week…[Uncle Pat] got tickets for us to go to Disneyland and Universal Studios. The visit was rather uneventful except for the hospitality we enjoyed. They had a cook/housekeeper who would take our orders for breakfast whenever we got up. Aunt Shelia was a beautiful lady and a grand hostess."

Much was going on in the world of television now. *The Beverly Hillbillies* had become such a rousing success that the networks wanted to make similar shows. Consequently, Pat received many offers for television series. He turned them down, feeling that his particular type of humor is best done as a supporting character, rather than being its central focus.

Then along came *Green Acres*.

Chapter Nine

Green Acres

They thought he would audition for the role of Eb, the hired hand. Pat found the part of Mr. Haney to be much more interesting, though. But, they pleaded, Mr. Haney is just a one-time deal. He'd just be in the first episode and nothing else. "We'll see," Pat said knowingly as he auditioned for Mr. Haney. Sure enough, the studio executives were charmed by his characterization of the lovable con man and gave him a permanent place in the series.

Green Acres began filming in the summer of 1965, in preparation for its fall debut on CBS. This thirty-minute situation comedy would be aired on Wednesdays at 9:00 p.m. Pat's co-stars in this charming show were Eddie Albert, Eva Gabor, Tom Lester, Alvy Moore, Mary Grace Canfield, Sid Melton, Frank Cady, and Hank Patterson. Some of the regulars from *Petticoat Junction* would sometimes show up, as well, since the two rural shows were both set in Hooterville. Creator/writer Jay Sommers and executive producer Paul Henning were the heart and soul behind this mega-hit.

Coincidentally, Pat was now working occasionally with Smiley Burnette, who had been Gene Autry's first sidekick. Smiley had the recurring role of Hooterville railroader Charlie Pratt in this series.

Kerry gives us the inside scoop: "*Green Acres* was a fun set. There were no prima donnas, no egos; just a well-coordinated group of professionals who knew how to write, direct and perform comedy. Dad fitted well into the way Jay Sommers and Dick Chevillat wrote. You see cornpone and expect that to be reflected in the dialogue, but what you get is a surprisingly sophisticated level of interaction. To be sure, there are running sight gags, such as Lisa's rubbery pancakes and the closet door that continually falls off its rails, but the dialogues between Eddie Albert and Alvy Moore or Eddie and Dad, achieved all of the intricacy and precision of any Marx Brothers or Abbott and Costello routine."

"*Green Acres*," Kerry continues, "was inhabited by characters and subsets of characters who had their own peculiar logic. Writers Chevillat and Sommers stuck with that logic and kept the comedy character-driven, rather than situation-driven. The situation, city fish in country pond, was established at the outset. From then on, the characters drove the show. The viewer would expect Oliver, who is so keen on becoming a farmer, to be the one who adapts most easily. However, it is Lisa in her designer dresses, who fits right in, accepting without effort the circuitous logic of the Hooterville denizens, establishing an easy rapport with one and all, even unto cows, chickens and pigs.

"It is Oliver who is flummoxed by life and farming in Hooterville. His careful study of scientific farming journals comes to naught in a community where Doris's lumbago determines which crops Fred Ziffel will plant.

"As Mr. Haney, my dad's part in all of this was to anticipate what Mr. Douglas would need or want next and have it on his truck by 6:00 a.m. Dad said he modeled his Mr. Haney character partly on Colonel Tom Parker, Elvis Presley's manager. Dad knew Elvis and the Colonel well, having made two pictures with Elvis and working often in Las Vegas.

"The *Green Acres* years were happy ones for Dad," says Kerry. "It was steady, home-for-dinner-every-night work and the show rated consistently in the Neilsen top ten."

"Eva Gabor was a doll, a sweetheart and a thoroughly professional actress," continues Kerry. "She was the same age as my mother and they started out at Fox together in the same 'class' of ingenues, studying under Max Reinhardt. I remember Mom told me Eva and Reinhardt worked like the devil to get rid of her Hungarian accent. It took a full six months and then it turned out she couldn't get a job WITHOUT the accent, so she 'reacquired' it.

"My first visit to the *Green Acres* set was when I was twelve or so. Eva held her arms out to me and said, "Oh, darling, you look just like your mother!" This was a sweet thing for her to say. At the time, I was all elbows, knees and glasses. She told me wonderful things about my mother and those first, exciting months at Fox, when just the words 'under contract at Fox' held magic that opened the doors to snooty shops in Beverly Hills and fine Hollywood eateries.

"Eva appeared on time each shooting day for her 5:00 a.m. make-up call. She wore comfortable clothes and no makeup to work and was completely unselfconscious about people seeing her that way. She sat patiently through the makeup and hair sessions and stood patiently through final costume fittings, chatting amiably with cast and crew alike. Then, she waited calmly for her call to the set. She stood, un-complaining, under hot studio lights while the scene movements were blocked out and light readings taken and then did her on-camera work with as much freshness as if she had just stepped in from a meadow in early spring. Not only did she have her lines down, she had an in-nate sense of comic timing that meshed precisely with Eddie's own tim-ing. Though there was no music involved, it was perfect pitch. Eva was amazing. Everyone loved her."

Regarding Eva, Buttram confided, "Well now, the thing about the Gabor gals is they know how to handle men, and that includes actors, directors, the crew. Eva smiles and all of us on the set, we just melt. She's something to see, that Miss Eva Gabor. I get to looking at her lines and I forget my own." It seems the admiration was mutual. In a five-page article about Pat in the October 22, 1966 issue of *TV Guide*, Eva proclaimed him "an absolute dear" as she mussed his hair affectionately.

In this same article, producer Jay Sommers said that Pat "is a com-fortable guy to be around," and Eddie Albert thought of him as a "price-less old shoe."

Musing about the show, and his part in it, Pat told Donald Freeman, TV-Radio editor of *The San Diego Union*, "It's catching on, this character I play in 'Green Acres.' I'm the country slicker, the rural con man, the bucolic Bilko. The kids especially take to this Mr. Haney fella I play. They have a healthy respect for larceny, kids do."

In his own way, though, Mr. Haney served as a shining example to kids. He always made sure to fasten his seatbelt before heading out in his pickup truck. True, the "seatbelt" was only a rope but, nevertheless, he always tied it on.

Pat wouldn't always stick completely to the script. His co-stars would remark later that he added so much to the show by using his own words sometimes.

Co-star Tom Lester, who played hired-hand Eb, had met Pat for the first time when the series began. "He was great to work with," Lester says of Pat. "His humor was on and off stage. When I hear his name, I think of how great a guy he was and how funny he was."

Of all the characters Pat played throughout his career, it was this one, Mr. Haney, that many people liked best. "For me," says Michael Alley, "he was one of the many high points of the show."

Mr. Haney was so much a part of Hooterville that he was asked to occasionally appear on *Petticoat Junction*. In the episode "County Fair," his character runs the booth in which the participant tries to win a prize with his pitching skills. When Betty Jo wins her selection of the goods on the shelf, of course, Mr. Haney, true to his nature, tries to interest her in the cheaper items—a Kewpie doll, a plastic horse, etc.—when what she really wants is the more-expensive tape recorder.

It came as a surprise to everyone when, after the 6th season, still in the top ten, *Green Acres* was canceled by CBS, along with every other country show. CBS wanted an image change. They wanted to be seen as a "hip, sophisticated network."

That was, of course, absurd. What could they have been thinking? "They cancelled everything with a tree," Pat commented, "including Lassie."

A couple decades later, Pat was still being interviewed about *Green Acres*, which never lost its enthusiastic audience. Happily, viewers are now able to get the show, a season at a time, on DVD. In an interview with *Times* staff reporter Katie Smith, Pat recalled one of his favorites of Mr. Haney's con jobs: "One time there was a farmer that had one cow and I sold him two milking machines. He didn't have any money, so I took the cow as a down payment," he laughed.

In hot pursuit of the bad guys, in Autry film *Barbed Wire*.
[from the collection of Kerry Galgano.]

He could always make Gene laugh. [From the collection of Kerry Galgano.]

[From the collection of
Kerry Galgano.]

Pat and Gene in the film *Apache Country*. [From the collection of
Kerry Galgano—photo by Lippman, Columbia Pictures.]

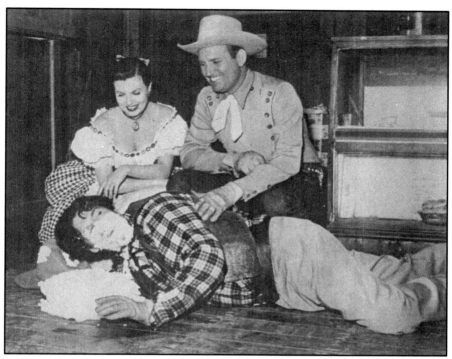

Sheila's dream job, from the television episode "Border Justice."
[From the collection of Kerry Galgano.]

An oversized postcard in tribute to the great westerns sidekicks.

Papa Buttram was very proud of Pat. [From the collection of Gus and Rebecca Buttram.]

From *Valley of Fire*. [From the collection of Kerry Galgano.]

Above and left:
Photo shoot, 1954.
[From the collection of
Kerry Galgano. Photos
by Robert Perkins.]

Waving bye-bye to his family
on the way to work.

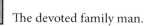

The devoted family man.

Having a little fun. He wouldn't really do it, would he?

Pat was an avid collector of books. On the walls are original paintings by Sheila. [From the collection of Kerry Galgano.]

Radio was always Pat's favorite form of broadcasting.

Pat is now officially "discovered" by Hedda Hopper. With them is his friend Arthur Godfrey. [From the collection of Kerry Galgano.]

Pat was a guest on Ed Sullivan's show several times.
[From the collection of Kerry Galgano.]

With Richard
Chamberlain.
[From the collection
of Kerry Galgano.]

With Claude Rains in *Twilight of Honor*. [From the collection of Kerry Galgano.]

From the 1965 *Castle of Frankenstein* magazine: "On set of
Hitchcock's The Jar, Pat Buttram tells co-star Collin Wilcox
and Jar author Ray Bradbury about his days with 'Gene Artery.'"

With Barbara Stanwyck on the set of *Roustabout*.
[From the collection of Kerry Galgano.]

Chapter Ten

When he could tear himself away from Hollywood, Pat would often go back home to Alabama. UPI Hollywood correspondent Vernon Scott reported that Pat made the trek to his Alabama cabin a couple times a year. At this three-room cabin, there was no plumbing or running water. "It's like Daniel Boone territory," he told Scott. "But I go back to loaf around, do some writing and thinking, and to talk to the natives. It keeps me in touch with the down-to-earth attitude that's absolutely necessary for me." Not only was that manna for his soul, but also crucial to his career. "I like being a country boy, and the minute I begin feeling like a city slicker, I run right off to Alabama."

By May 1966, when this article was run, Pat was appearing at about three benefits each week. He didn't expect payment for these events, wanting the money to go to the charities instead.

"Dad was generous to a fault, as the saying goes," says daughter Kerry. "People who admired something of his were likely to end up taking it home with them. It made him happy to give—to be able to give. I think childhood poverty impressed him mightily."

His generosity extended to his brothers and sisters as well. "When Uncle Gus started having trouble getting around," Kerry says, "Dad sent him a golf cart to wander around Camp Maxwell in. [Camp Maxwell, built by Gus on the property in the Pebble Community near Haleyville that had once belonged to his grandparents, was a camp for children with disabilities.] He sent Aunt Peggy a magnifying light to help her do her craft work more easily. Aunt Peggy was an artist. Like Aunt Hallie, her medium was flowers. Hallie is a world-class flower arranger, which he encouraged."

"We were checking out some wooded property once," Hallie says, "and he found some wood he thought I could use in my flower arrangements. He was real observant and appreciative of beauty all around him." Peggy made greeting cards—lovely compositions of pressed flowers, enhanced with her drawings. She had a lively business selling her cards and was always swamped with orders. Pat would never fail to send his brothers and sisters Christmas gifts that were tailor-made for their needs or interests. Often, he would give them presents for no special reason other than the fact that he found something that was just perfect for the receiver. Sister Mamie enjoyed making Raggedy Ann dolls for people, so Pat bought her a book about the history of Raggedy Anns.

Once summer arrived, nineteen-year-old Mac Buttram wanted to go visit his famous relatives again, so he, his cousin Mike, and Mike's friend Jimbo drove westward in a pickup truck with a camper on the back. "We also stayed with Uncle Pat, Aunt Sheila, and Kerry about a week. Uncle Pat got us tickets to Disneyland, Universal Studios, an L.A. Dodgers game, and an exhibition NFL game in Anaheim. Probably the highlight of that trip was Uncle Pat taking us to the set of *The Andy Griffith Show*, where we met Andy, 'Floyd,' and 'Goober.' When Uncle Pat told George Lindsey Mike was from Jasper, George said, 'Andy, these boys are from Jaaasper.' We saw a segment of the show filmed that I see from time to time today. Uncle Pat also bought our lunch at the Universal Studios cafeteria, where we met Al Lewis, who was playing 'Grandpa Munster' at the time. He also took us to the famous Brown Derby restaurant, where we met Don Adams of *Get Smart*."

"Like Gene, Pat knew everybody in the world," says Johnny Western. "He could talk to anybody on their level. He could talk to some hillbilly from a shotgun shack in Arkansas just as easily as he could talk to a governor or a senator. Everybody loved Pat."

"It was a great trip," continues Mac, "and I again enjoyed the hospitality of Aunt Shelia and the cook/housekeeper. We boys thought we were really something staying at a movie star's house, swimming in his pool, and ordering breakfast from the cook whenever we got up each morning. Aunt Sheila called us 'my boys.'" Mac would eventually become the lucky recipient of a Kawasaki motorcycle that Pat had been given at a trade show.

Even though this environment might have seemed "Hollywood" to the average person, Pat worked hard to provide as normal a lifestyle as possible for his family. By Southern California standards, his home was rather simple. They were living in a small college town, with college professors for neighbors. Their home was like numberless others that were built throughout the country during the post-WWII era—a ranch-style tract home. Ostentatious living was not his style.

→ ←

Pat's Pearls of Wisdom

"Why do they let a funeral procession go through red lights? What's the hurry?"

→ ←

Pat appeared with Eva Gabor, Eddie Albert, Jim Nabors, Wayne Newton, and The Young Americans at the 1967 Grand National All Star Spectacular Rodeo/Horse Show at the Cow Palace in San Francisco. At this and many other on-the-road shows, Pat would give fans autographed photos of himself as Mr. Haney.

"You all have pictures?" he asked the dozen-or-so young fans.

"Yes," they assured him.

Once satisfied that all were served, he held out his hand in true Mr. Haney fashion. "That'll be thirty cents apiece." The result was gales of laughter.

Beverly Taliaferro remembers that day very well. "My cousin and I were waiting in the back for Eva [Gabor] to come out when Pat asked us if we would like his autograph. We promptly asked him 'Who are you?' He said, 'Well, I'm Pat Buttram.' Of course, our next sentence was, "Who's Pat Buttram?' Well, he explained and then signed his picture in our souvenir book. A very nice man."

He also made a personal appearance farther up the state at Shasta County's Sheriff's Posse Rodeo in Redding. The hospitality he received there was quite gratifying.

Pat just loved these personal appearances because of the live audiences. Hearing their laughter brought joy to his heart.

His *Green Acres* image followed him everywhere. He was a guest star on two episodes of the comedy *Pistols 'n' Petticoats*. Traces of Mr. Haney could be seen in his character in the 1967 episode "The Golden Fleece." This is a story of Jake Turner (Pat's character), a country man who, upon release from prison, is determined to go straight. It breaks his family's hearts when he decides to leave the family business (robbery) to become an honest land agent. He tries so hard, but is tempted once too often and reverts back to his scheming ways, much to the relief of his family. Complete with mustache and long beard, Pat looked very backwoods in this show, and delivered a delightful performance.

Artist Benny Yates sketched a portrait of Pat that appeared on the cover of *The Birmingham News'* November 18, 1967 "Punch" entertainment supplement. The magazine also carried an article about his coming appearance at the Toy Bowl.

Back at home in the Northridge section of the San Fernando Valley, their home now had a fish pond that contained tropical fish. Sheila had decorated the house in French provincial style with blue and green furnishings. In this home, too, Pat's den was his sanctuary; it was filled with books, plaques, a record player, television set, and tape recorders. Sheila could cook, but preferred for their housekeeper/cook to do it. "In the summer, we do a lot of outdoors cooking," Pat told Scott. "Guess who gets to wear the cute apron and the chef's hat?" The family pet was Chu-Chu, the Siamese cat. It had become a favorite family tradition to have parties to celebrate holidays. Sheila worked hard to make these parties wonderful, planning the meals far in advance and decorating the house so that it was perfect.

On April 4 of this year, Pat was the emcee of the Ronald Reagan roast. These were the roasts that he enjoyed the most. He was already a friend of the Reagans, and his good-natured ribbing kept them all in stitches. While Pat appeared on a few of the televised *Dean Martin Celebrity Roasts*, he didn't consider them bona fide. There was more artistic freedom at the true, untelevised ones, in which he was able to write all of his own material. That's when the real laughs began.

Did he ever get in trouble for the jokes he made about any of the politicians? You bet he did! Whenever a politician would complain about a joke, Pat would make up for it by writing one for him, then all would be forgiven.

George Burns was legendary for his pranks, especially on his hapless pal Jack Benny. He pulled one on Pat, as well. Pat was scheduled to talk to a group but, before going on, George casually asked him what he does with his hands as he's speaking. Never having given it much thought, Pat didn't know what to tell him. "That's okay," said George. "I'll be in the audience and I'll be watching to see what you do with your hands." Needless to say, Pat's hand movements weren't their most natural that evening. Being uncharacteristically self-conscious, Pat glanced over at George during his speech and found him puffing his cigar with a big grin.

In order to keep abreast of the country lifestyle, Pat subscribed to more than fifty rural newspapers. He sent tapes of his radio broadcasts to prison deejays, and they sent him their own newspapers in return, which he also enjoyed.

As was a family tradition, Pat belonged to the Masons, the oldest fraternal organization in the world. This philanthropic group is dedicated to "the Brotherhood of Man under the Fatherhood of God."

He had much admiration for Abraham Lincoln and Will Rogers, and was always on the lookout for the writings of Ambrose Bierce. His hobbies were different from most people's. He had a huge collection of buttonhooks. This was an accidental collection. He had jokingly told a reporter once that he collected them. When the resulting article hit print, its readers began sending him buttonhooks left over from their childhood or that they had found in antique stores. He soon had a fine collection.

Collections he maintained intentionally were coins and sheet music. He bought rare copies of music for a very good, very unselfish reason: "You take someone like Arthur Godfrey," he told *Syracuse Herald-American* reporter Joan E. Vadeboncoeur. "He's got everything. But I can give him this (an original copy of a song he introduced) and it's something he doesn't have and would have trouble finding." Pat would catalogue his music collection, enabling him to find a specific piece quickly. Daughter Kerry would sometimes work with him on his collections.

Pat frequently browsed bookstores, as well. Gilbert's Books at Hollywood & Vine had the perfect tome for his buddy, Hal Kanter. It was titled simply *Clowns*, and Pat bought it, inscribing it, "To Hal who woulda made a great clown-writer. Easy, Pat Buttram," and presented it to the writer of wit. There was plenty in bookstores of interest to himself, as well. He was fascinated by literature that dealt with covered bridges, barns, and Egyptian Archeology. While in southern Illinois, which is rich in Lincoln lore, Pat had developed an avid interest in the Civil War. His knowledge of the war and that era was vast, and Pat and his brother Johnny had enjoyed debating strategies. "It was almost like they were reliving the war," recalls niece Harriet.

⇝　⇜

Regarding Johnny Carson: "He's an Episcopalian—that's an Off-Broadway Catholic."

Regarding Disneyland: "It's the first people trap ever built by a mouse."

Regarding Milton Berle: "Milton recently switched from comedy to drama. Unfortunately, it happened while he was still doing comedy."

Regarding being among big stars speaking at the Friars Club: "I'm the only one here tonight I haven't heard of."

⋙   ⋘

Pat was given his own show in the mid-1960s over the radio station KGBS in Los Angeles. "He did comedy vignettes that lasted into early 1969. We became great friends," recalls radio staffer Bob Morgan. "He began his vignettes when KGBS was country, prior to going 'Now Sound' in 1968. Ron Erwin was the program director then and wanted to cancel Pat, but the general manager, Dale Peterson, insisted on keeping Pat to the end of his contract." He would come in once a week to record his vignettes for the next week.

Pat was wanted at the cinema, as well. In the 1968 film *I Sailed to Tahiti with an All Girl Crew*, Gardner McKay and Fred Clark were the main stars, while Pat provided the subplot. The two men are racing to Tahiti, and McKay has a crew of five beautiful women and one teenaged stowaway. At every port, there is Buttram, looking for someone. It isn't clear at first if he is the good guy or the bad guy. Turns out he is the Pooler County sheriff, whose mission is to capture a criminal onboard. While the movie in general was light fare, the humor came from practically every character except the sheriff.

⋙   ⋘

The Hollywood Reporter announced that Pat was the "most thefted comic of them all," but that it didn't bother him in the least. "Pat Buttram is probably the most quoted comic around town since Joe Frisco," it reported on April 2, 1968. "And at writer's rates he could probably make a fortune. But his gags are either stolen or given away free. 'How can you charge your friends?' Pat asked with a shrug of his football player size shoulders. 'You don't think about things like that.'" While he was known to kid just about everyone in the business, only one person seems to have taken offense. As a result, he received an angry telegram from Jerry Lewis.

➤   ➤

Word went out to the Hollywood community that its help was needed. Fifteen-year-old Marianne Baratta was dying of kidney disease, but her life might be saved if money could be raised for dialysis treatment while a new kidney was being sought. Dialysis and the transplant would cost $40,000, money the Baratta family did not have.

Friends and neighbors had done what they could, holding bake sales and school rallies. Governor Reagan had sent her a check and a jar of jellybeans. Those things were wonderful, but more money was needed.

Movie stars are often stereotyped as self-absorbed and spoiled, but their reaction to this crisis knocked that stereotype on its ear. Clamoring to help was Barbara Stanwyck, Elvis Presley, Julie Andrews, John Wayne, Johnny Grant, Lawrence Welk, Bobby Burgess, Angela Cartwright, Brendon Boone, Deborah Walley, Jon Provost, and many more. Stars signed autographs for a dollar each. A movie-star auction was held, and Pat was very happy to serve as the auctioneer for this very worthy cause. Money started rolling in. The highest bid came for Elvis' own shirt. A landowner in Las Vegas, who had just sold property to Howard Hughes, made a large donation as well. With the help of these angels-on-earth, the goal had finally been met.

A year later, Marianne was back in school and living a more normal life. She was well on her way to recovery. This, Pat told the reporter, was the answer to their prayers.

➤   ➤

While Pat would attend, his pal Gene Autry was usually missing at friends' and associates' funerals. That was because Autry wanted to avoid such unpleasantness whenever possible. He told Pat once, "Now look, let's make a promise. I'm not going to your funeral and I don't want you to come to mine." Pat responded with a straight face, "Well, Gene, I'm afraid we can't work it that way. It has to go one way or t'other." That lightened Autry's troubled mood.

➤   ➤

Pat might not have been a superstar, but that was fine by him. "Stars get out of work, but sidekicks go on forever," he told Birmingham reporter Turner Jordan.

While he had already been busy with *Green Acres* and charity dinners, Pat had agreed to write a humorous column for a California newspaper. It was called "Pat Buttram Sez," and would appear on their front page. He'd arise at 4:00 a.m. to do this, so it wouldn't interfere with his regular workday. "Immediately it became one of the most popular columns in the *Hollywood Citizen-News* and *Valley Times* and it is now syndicated with the Editor's Workshop Syndicate," that newspaper proudly reported in June 1969. By October, Pat's column was carried by over thirty newspapers throughout the country, including *The Birmingham News*. "It's the most challenging thing I've done," Pat told the Hollywood reporter in an article also run in Birmingham. "To make people laugh on television or at a club is one thing. But to do it just with words is a lot tougher, because you can't use gestures and facial expression." Even so, he was quite effective.

Also, in June of 1969, Pat signed a three-year contract with the Bonanza Hotel for over $400,000. This was a new hotel and they wanted to offer topnotch entertainment. Pat was to serve as an official ambassador and host, and perform on-stage at least twenty weeks per year. This was prior to *Green Acres'* cancellation so he was also working regularly on that show, plus writing the syndicated newspaper column.

The *Hollywood Citizen-News* loved Pat so much that they would later devote an entire page to him, titling it "That Lovable 'Green Acres' Guy." Consisting of fourteen photos of him at various stages of his career, this tribute spotlighted the many facets of his talent: as humorist, after-dinner speaker, goodwill ambassador, movie-TV star, and newspaper columnist. He was shown with not only his family, but also with many of the greats of the day: George Burns, Bob Hope, Jimmy Durante, Jack Benny, Dean Martin, Phil Harris, Dorothy Lamour, Bing Crosby, Cara Williams and Joey Bishop. Pat had worked with or at least appeared at functions with them all. This article served to illustrate the fact that he had come a very long way since his Alabama days.

During Pat's visit to Alabama that year, he made a special point to go see Camp Maxwell, the children's camp that he and Gus established. "I love the place," Pat said. "We have lodges, waterfalls, caves and it's just a Mark Twain-type place."

⇛   ⇚

Pat had met Walt Disney earlier, and now Disney realized the Buttram voice could add a lot to his animated films. Chosen by the head man himself, Pat appeared in his first of many Disney productions in 1969. It was called *The Aristocats*. He, along with friends George Lindsey, Eva Gabor, and Phil Harris, as well as Sterling Holloway, Nancy Culp, and other notable actors, supplied the voices of the animated characters. As brother Gus would tell the *Times Daily*, "Walt Disney loved Pat and that southern drawl of his. He told Pat one time that he had one of the most distinctive voices he'd ever heard in his life." Indeed, Disney said that the only other person who had such a recognizable voice was Orson Welles. Welles then confided to Buttram, "You know that means we can't ever make obscene phone calls."

Doing voice work for Disney came naturally for Pat because of his radio training. Some actors, however, found it quite difficult to portray a character entirely with their voices, rather than using physical means of expression. One thing Pat liked about working for this company was that they did not enhance or change the recorded voices at all. What the audience heard was the dialogue exactly as it was recorded by the voice actor.

Animated Disney films are much more difficult to create than most viewers realize. They were of the ultimate quality; no expense was spared. Each one took four years to make because the voices would be recorded first, then each frame would be hand-drawn to fit both the words being said and the personality of the person saying them. You can see some of Pat's physical traits in his animated characters. In this particular movie, Eva Gabor is the voice of the gentle, loving mama cat named "Duchess," George Lindsey and Pat are dogs named Napoleon and Lafayette. Were the two men in the building recording their lines at the same time, or was it done separately and pieced together later? "We recorded together," says Lindsey. "We only worked like one day every six months." Sterling Holloway is their mouse friend, "Roquefort." It was Phil Harris' voice that gave tomcat Thomas J. O'Malley life as he gallantly rescues Duchess and her three kittens and leads them home. This film incorporated adventure, humor, romance, music, and bad-guys and good-guys to tell us an endearing story. The artwork is breathtaking, as well. As the story wound up, it was Pat's hound dog character who haughtily tells his companion dog, "*I'm* the leader! *I'll* say when it's the end. (long pause) It's the end." *The Aristocats* was the last full-length animated movie that received Walt Disney's personal stamp of approval. Unfortunately, he didn't live long enough to see it in its finished form.

Over the years, Pat had lent his services to brother John's radio station WJBY in Gadsden whenever he was in the area. Too, he had appeared on their "Dixie Jamboree" at the city auditorium frequently during the 1940s. To express their appreciation for all this, the city set aside a day in January 1970, as "Pat Buttram Day."

It appears Jasper, Alabama had the same idea. Says Mac, "Uncle Pat came to Jasper (the county that joins Winston County to the south, also the home of George 'Goober' Lindsey) when we lived there. They had a 'Pat Buttram Day,' making Uncle Pat an honorary citizen and presenting him with the key to the city. His line, when he received the key, was, 'Now they are going to change all the locks.'

"There was a variety show with Uncle Pat as the headliner. Before and after the show people who said they knew Daddy [Gus] and Uncle Pat when they were growing up were all around. They would talk to Daddy first, then he would 'turn them over' to Uncle Pat with the line, 'Pat, you know who this is.' Uncle Pat finally told Daddy, 'Gus, quit sending these folks to me saying, 'You know who this is'—I don't know any of them. Tell me their names.' Daddy said, 'I don't know them either.'

"Also on that trip, the local Lincoln-Mercury dealer, Carl Price, let the city borrow a Lincoln Continental to chauffer Uncle Pat around. My older cousin, John Wilson Buttram (Uncle Johnny's son), was the chauffer. Uncle Pat stayed at the Warrior River Motel, about 8 miles south of town. I rode with John Wilson when we took Uncle Pat back to the motel. We left him there and ran out of gas on the way back to Jasper. It took us a long time to get someone to get us going again. We were real classy—a 'limo,' but couldn't afford to put gas in it."

Pat's sister Hallie kept a scrapbook of Pat's many films and other activities. He was so proud of that. Many of the photos included in this book come from Hallie's scrapbook.

The next month, Vernon Scott, of the United Press International in Hollywood, wrote an article entitled "Hayseed Slicker an Actor With Considerable Wisdom." The discrepancy Pat demonstrated intrigued him. He wrote, "Beneath guileless eyes and a voice that would etch glass, Buttram is a man of considerable wisdom, all the while hiding behind the façade of a bumpkin." Some of Pat's biggest fans, he stated, were teenagers, which didn't surprise Pat at all. "I think it's because of the character I play in the television show," he told the reporter. "Mr. Haney is anti-establishment. He's always getting the best of his social superiors."

Pat was very much appreciated by many charities, too, for his tireless efforts on their behalf. The Los Angeles Press Club banquet in the fall of 1970 was held in his honor. That night, he received not just one, but many awards from several different institutions. "I remember meeting Pat O'Brien, one of my favorite actors, that night at the Press Club," says Kerry. "He and Dad were good friends."

President Richard Nixon was not able to attend, but he sent a letter with a certificate, praising Pat's charitable and civic works.

By example and word, he taught daughter Kerry to pass along any good fortune that comes her way.

It was during this era that Pat recorded an album, *Pat Buttram... We Wuz Poor*. Endorsed by Lorne Greene, this album was recorded live at the Palomino Nightclub in North Hollywood. On it, we hear demonstrated Pat's humor on topics such as commercials, poverty, Gene Autry, *Green Acres*, and kids. One joke he told was that, at his age, birth control pills serve to help one to sleep. *Sleep?* Why, yes! Put one in your teenaged daughter's orange juice each morning, and you'll sleep like a log.

Pat received two special Emmy awards, as well. Rather than statuettes, special Emmys were discs. He was given one bronze and one silver one in recognition of his services to the Academy of Television Arts & Sciences. In October 1970, he was also given the Conquistadores Award from the Bullock's San Fernando Valley. People everywhere appreciated Pat.

⇥   ⇤

It seemed that, whenever people were photographed with Pat in a candid shot, everyone in the picture was laughing. An example of this could be found in the January 1971 issue of *TV Picture Life* magazine. A photo in Jane Ardmore's "Hollywood Beat" column shows Pat, Eva Gabor, and her husband, Richard Brown, enjoying a joke to the fullest.

Among the people for whom Pat was writing now was Gov. Ronald Reagan, whom he had known since Reagan's sports-announcer days. "What I write for the governor are little observations," Pat told Copley News Service reporter Don Freeman. "Like, for instance: If a man holds you up with a registered gun and you shoot him with a gun that isn't registered, you're in more trouble than he is." Another of Reagan's favorite Buttram lines was "All the people in favor of abortion are already born."

Pat also wrote for Ken "Festus" Curtis. Curtis would use the material when he went out on the fair and rodeo circuit. A quote Pat gave him was "Beauty is only skin deep but ugly goes clear to the bone." Curtis used some of Pat's material in his record album, *Gunsmoke's Festus Sings 'n Talks 'bout Dodge City 'n Stuff.* Sometimes Gene Autry needed a light-hearted opener for a speech. Pat would come to his rescue and write one for him. Other stars who benefitted from Buttram jokes were Phil Harris, Jimmy Dean, Andy Griffith, George Lindsey, and Karl Malden.

He also wrote a baseball joke book, which was selling very well at ballparks all over the country. "I've got a line in the book I first said about the New York Mets when they were so bad. I said that the Mets play like a box of Kleenex—they're soft and gentle and they pop up one at a time." Or how about this one: "Question: What's the most common triple play in baseball? Answer: Mustard—to hot dog—to somebody's lap."

Pat's mind was sharp and he was always coming up with ideas. It wasn't unusual for him to get one of those ideas in the middle of the night. Imagination seems to be at its best sometimes in that twilight area between waking and sleeping. At such times, Pat would grab the ever-present pad and pencil and write it down so it wouldn't be lost.

⇛   ⇚

Pat's Pearl of Wisdom

Regarding Dean Martin: "Dean would eat hay if you dipped it in gin."

Regarding Bob Hope: "Doesn't this guy have terrible jobs? While we're home at Christmas watching the kids fighting over the toys and knocking over the tree, Bob is in the Pacific with Raquel Welch."

Regarding Mae West: "Do you realize that she went through her life without once having a man say to her, 'You remind me of my mother'?"

⇛   ⇚

Larry Belanger, who wrote for the *Mountain Democrat* in Placerville, California, filled his "Words and Music" column with Buttramisms in the October 30, 1971 issue. He, like everyone else, loved to quote the humorist. Here is a sample of that day's column:

PAT BUTTRAM SEZ:

I don't know if you know it or not, but I come from a town that's so small they don't even have a sanitation department...just a woman who comes in twice a week to tidy up.

Statistics show that at age 70 there are five women to every man...a great time for a guy to get those odds.

In the early 1970s, Pat was making appearances, as usual, around the country. Writes Jim Ciardi, "Pat Buttram made a live appearance on the grandstand stage at the Del Mar Fair. I, along with my family, was in the audience that night. The grandstand was packed. He came out in his 'Mr. Haney' costume...and, I swear, the grandstand collapsed!!!! I mean the crowd went *wild*!!! I don't remember anything about his act other than it was what we today call a stand-up routine, and it was about the funniest show I have ever seen."

➤   ◄

Pat's agent, William Loeb, was busy at work and, once again, Pat was cast among other well-known voices in a Disney production that was released in 1973. Its title was *Robin Hood*, and each animated character was an animal with human qualities: Robin Hood (voiced by Brian Bedford) was a fox, Maid Marian (Monica Evans) a vixen, Prince John (Peter Ustinov) a lion, Sir Hiss (Terry-Thomas) a snake, Little John (Phil Harris) a bear, Friar Tuck (Andy Devine) a badger, the Sheriff of Nottingham (Pat Buttram) a wolf, and vultures Trigger (George Lindsey) and Nutsy (Ken Curtis). The story was narrated by a minstrel-rooster (Roger Miller). Miller had written a few songs for this movie and performed them as the narrator.

When questioned by Little John about the fact that they are stealing from the rich to give to the poor, Robin Hood corrects him—they are just borrowing, not stealing. Bad guys Prince John and Sir Hiss are plotting to not only tax the poor townsfolk mercilessly, but also to capture and kill Robin Hood. Buttram's sheriff character is also a bad guy, taking delight in collecting for the prince all the money he can squeeze out of the subjects—even a child's birthday present and the contents of the church's poor box. But, alas, the prince's plans for ridding the world of Robin Hood are for naught. Hood is too clever for them and has too many friends, including King Richard.

Most viewers today are most taken by the humor of this version. There are, indeed, some golden lines in it, mostly spoken by Little John and the bad guys. Viewers don't even mind the southern accents of the sheriff, Trigger and Nutsy in the British town of Nottingham. Many proclaim this their all-time favorite reenactment of the Robin Hood story, some saying it's even the best Disney movie ever. The music was exceptional.

Just before *Robin Hood*, Pat appeared in person (not an animated voice) in another film, *The Gatling Gun* (1972). The story revolves around possession of the title lethal weapon, which Cavalry troops have initially. Will they keep it or will the Apaches gain access to it in order to protect their land Appearing with him in this movie was Guy Stockwell, Robert Fuller, Barbara Luna, Patrick Wayne, John Carradine, and Phil Harris. Pat's very likable character was called "Tin Pot," and he was a wealth of information. For instance, did you know that a doctor invented the Gatling gun for the purpose of making war so gosh-awful that people would give up and stop fighting? Tin Pot also knew how to fix the weapon, and he even comes in handy for translating for his comrades when an Indian speaks to them in Spanish.

One scene has special significance to anyone who knows Pat's history. He was positioned behind the powerful, freestanding Gatling gun and began firing it. Did this bring back unpleasant memories to him of a similar stunt that went awry back in 1950? If it did, one wouldn't know it. Pat played this scene like the seasoned pro he was.

This picture was filmed on two ranches in New Mexico, and each actor had his own cabin for the six weeks it took. Robert Fuller laughs when remembering those days. His cabin in Santa Fe was between those of Pat and Phil Harris. Professionally, he found Pat to be protective, supportive, and quite experienced. "He never missed a line," Fuller recalls. "He was the consummate actor, and very smart. He knew his dialog. He had his character down."

Once the cameras were turned off, though, Pat kept everyone laughing. "He was fun, and Phil was, too. We had a great time." And when you put Pat together with Phil Harris, anything can happen. It seems that

Fuller was introduced to the concept of a scotch-and-milk breakfast by his fellow actors.

→   ←

These years were quite fruitful for Pat, not only because of the abundance of work, but also for personal reasons: "Dad and I reconnected when I was an adult," says Gayle, "and we had many wonderful conversations by phone as well as writing to each other."

What a blessing it was to have communication with his elder daughter reestablished. She wasn't "gone forever" from him after all.

→   ←

In an episode of *Love, American Style*, "Love and the Competitors," Pat was teamed up with a fellow *Green Acres* regular—Tom Lester. The elder man played the police chief and Lester was his deputy, as they dealt with a young drag-racing duo, whose fierce competitiveness had them each trying to one-up the other throughout the night.

Then Pat was emceeing a film festival of Ray Webb's movies in Memphis in 1974 when he met a man who would become a very good friend. His name was Jim Rorie. Their friendship, like all of Pat's friendships, would last the rest of their lives, and he would call Jim at least once a week. Jim chuckles when he thinks back on a charity benefit honoring General Chuck Yaeger. No one wanted to follow Pat. Anything after his monologue would be an anticlimax. Once, when Jim was in the area, staying at the Sherman Oaks Inn, Pat called to see if they could get together. Jim agreed, and Pat came to pick him up. Jim was in cowboy garb and Pat was in a tuxedo. Turns out he was doing a B'nai B'rith benefit that evening. Dressed as he was, Jim was afraid of looking out of place at such a grand event, so Pat took him to the Playboy Club down the street and told the ladies to take good care of him until he got back. As soon as the benefit was over, Pat returned and the two men enjoyed the rest of the evening together.

Jim laughingly recalls walking down a Los Angeles street with Pat and a few other men, and they began crossing to the other side. They must have been jaywalking, however, because soon they were stopped by a policeman. Eyes wide with innocence, Pat asked, "How fast were we going, officer?" The officer laughed and let them go.

At the time, Jim was working for Delta Airlines in Memphis. His boss was retiring and Jim asked Pat if he'd come and entertain at the retirement party. Pat came as Mr. Haney, and a real pig was furnished as part of his act. They had a huge turnout. Delta wanted to pay him but, instead, Pat asked if he could have a car for his brother Gus. They were pleased to comply.

It was during this year that Pat guest-starred on an episode of the popular television series *Emergency!* Entitled "The Floor Brigade," the story focused on a hermit (Buttram) who is trapped inside a cave after an avalanche. The firemen have to get past a Benji-like dog first. Once they subdue the dog and dig their way into the cave, they find the hermit still alive but unconscious. They pull him out, where he becomes semiconscious, and he asks, "This going to cost me anything?" The rescuers reassure him that it won't cost him a cent. Soon, we see him in the hospital, enjoying the hospital food and asking for seconds. The show had a happy ending—the manager of the supermarket, at which the hermit would regularly search the trash for food, offers to share his home with him.

Another show on which Pat appeared was the second *Milton Berle's Mad World of Comedy* special, filmed at the Masquers Club. In this show, Berle analyzes comedy with his guests, Dick Martin, Mort Sahl, Eddie Quillan, and Pat. Berle introduces Pat by telling us that showbiz insiders know him as the "Plato of the plow" and the "Mort Sahl of the fertilizer set." His guest assures him that he's as happy to be there as a cat following a leaky cow. What are the rules of rural humor, Berle asked. The most vital rule, Pat replied, was that the comedian must stay out of the bedroom. That doesn't mean sex jokes are taboo, however. As an example, he told the joke about the zebra from the circus getting loose and finding itself in the unfamiliar world of the barnyard. She asked the various animals there what they were and what they did. When she got to the bull, the answer she got was "Take off those crazy striped pajamas and I'll *show* you what I do."

Pat's appearance on this show gives the audience a rare glimpse of the real Pat Buttram. While he tried to be accommodating to his host, it seemed he was not really interested in analyzing anything. Once he began telling a joke, however, his face lit up and he was finally enjoying himself.

Pat's Pearls of Wisdom

about the space program

We spent a billion or so dollars to find out if there's intelligent life on Mars. I can tell you, yes, there is intelligent life on Mars 'cause they haven't spent one cent to find out about us.

I'll admit that scientists have come a long way. They can correct a malfunction in a space capsule millions of miles up in the sky. But I notice that the TV repairman still has to take my set to the shop every time to fix it.

The astronauts left an eight million dollar car on the moon, and brought home a bag of rocks. That's the same deal I got when I traded my car in at Cal's used car dealer.

➤   ◄

The *Las Vegas Sun* ran a front-page article about Pat on Valentine's Day of 1975. He was now appearing with Dick Haymes at the Thunderbird Hotel and Casino. Pat was by now "one of the most quoted men in Hollywood," it said. Apparently, in Las Vegas, too. Their shows took place at 8:00 P.M. for the dinner crowd and midnight for the night owls.

A couple months later Pat was showering one day when he slipped and fell. His hand went through the glass door and the small finger of his left hand was cut almost completely off. They rushed him to the hospital, but the news was bad: his finger could not be saved. Instead of the usual type of amputation, however, Pat asked them to remove the entire series of bones from that finger down to the wrist. This was done, and the missing finger was hardly noticeable as a result.

November 4, 1975 was probably the saddest day of Pat's life. That was the day he lost his beloved Sheila. He and Sheila had taken a Mexican cruise three years earlier, and she had contracted a lung infection there. That had necessitated many months of hospitalization and the removal of the affected lung. The infection eventually cleared up, but she later contracted cancer in her only remaining lung. The poor lady didn't have a chance. She soon succumbed.

Friends and relatives gathered around to console Pat. "Daddy [Gus] and I flew out there to be with Uncle Pat and Kerry and attend the services," says Mac. "Jim Davis, a western star from way back and of *Dallas* fame, was with Uncle Pat a lot during that time." Indeed, Davis understood grief all too well. His sixteen-year-old daughter Tara had died in a car accident only five years earlier.

"Daddy conducted the memorial service for Aunt Sheila," Mac continues. "As I recall, we met Eva Gabor, Tom 'Eb' Lester, and Alvy 'Mr. Kimball' Moore. Uncle Pat was having a very difficult time then."

It was rumored that Pat had a stroke shortly after his wife died. This was not true. "Dad never had a stroke in his life," declares daughter Kerry. "He missed her until the day he died and never remarried, but personal heartache never stopped him from working." Work, in fact, probably provided the distraction he needed to get on with life.

For their first Thanksgiving without Sheila, Pat and Kerry went to Alabama to spend the holiday with Gus and Becky.

➤　◄

It would have been insensitive of them to extend this invitation then, so they let some time lapse first. Then Pat was asked to entertain at the Alabama Funeral Directors Convention on June 21, 1977. The event took place in Point Clear, way at the southwestern tip of the state. He obliged, much to AFD president Red Nichols' delight. The sponsor was Aurora Casket Company, and the promotional sheet showed Pat on Boot Hill with his hand resting on a tombstone. Can you guess the topic of his jokes for that occasion?

The following month, he was on the cover of *Petersen's CB Life* magazine, with a nice article about him inside.

It was around this time that he and Harry Carey, Jr., were introduced and became friends. Carey had known of him for years, having attended some of the events he emceed. "He was the funniest master of ceremonies I've ever seen in my life," he says. "I've seen the legends back in the days with my dad, but I never saw one as good as Pat was. As an emcee, his timing was awesome!" Carey adds, "I enjoyed his company very much. He was a delightful man." The two would eventually make a couple of films together.

Pat's friendship with Gene Autry was still as strong as ever. They would get together once or twice a week.

The gift-giving continued. Kerry recalls, "When I was grown up, Dad enjoyed giving me things for my apartment or taking me clothes shopping."

Was Pat difficult to shop for? What sort of things did he like? "The answer is simple: TOYS!" she says. "Anything electronic fascinated him. The Sharper Image sales force rubbed their palms together when they saw him come in the door. He always came home with radios, clap lamps, robots, tiny TV sets, slippers with flashlights in the toes, talking alarm clocks…If it beeped, booped, lit up or moved, it followed him home."

In a group, however, Pat was said to have been rather shy. He was much more comfortable dealing with people one-on-one. On stage, he was at his best.

Pat's hard work in the broadcasting media earned him the Pacific Pioneer Broadcasters' highest honor, the Carbon Mike Award, on September 15, 1978. This took place at a luncheon at the Sportsmen's Lodge in Studio City, California, and was attended by over eight hundred people. Gene Autry, Arthur Godfrey, and Tex Williams were there, and Pat's good friend Hal Kanter served as host. Also on the dais with him were Eva Gabor and Phil Harris. Jeanne De Vivier Brown's job was to book the talent for such shows, and it just amazed her that Pat could go up to the mike with only a few key words written on the back of a grimy envelope and, from that, deliver a brilliant five-minute monolog. Attendees to Buttram events would often bring tape recorders so they wouldn't miss anything he said.

The Pacific Pioneer Broadcasters' archivist, Marty Halperin, recalls a project that Pat had suggested. It would be a record album of his speeches and would be called, "PB [Pat Buttram] at the PPB [Pacific Pioneer Broadcasters]." Marty liked that idea and later sent him a copy of the luncheon monologs he had videotaped. After viewing them, Pat shelved the idea, feeling that those performances were geared to the individual audiences and, thus, might not be fully understood by the general public.

The same month that Pat received the PPB award, *Hollywood Studio Magazine* put out a special edition, "The Comedians." Inside, Pat is pictured with Danny Thomas in a country scene and, on page 18, Sheila is surrounded by the Three Stooges in a scene from the film *Gold Raiders*.

Soon, there would be a new movie out with Pat in the cast, *Angels' Brigade*, which had a Charlie's Angels-like storyline. A high-school teacher is determined to bust a drug-producing compound that is ruining the lives of some of her students. She enlists the help of five other women—a police officer, a stuntwoman, a model, a karate instructor, and one of her students. Each woman uses her area of expertise to further their goal and, together, they destroy the drug source. Intimidating, as the head honchos of their foe, are Peter Lawford and Jack Palance. There are a lot of explosions and shootings—much work for the movie's stuntmen. Pat's one scene, however, was a refreshing break from the painful story. He played the car salesman who sells the ladies a monster-sized van that is soon to be recalled. His Mr. Haney image was still alive and well.

A tribute was paid to Shirley Temple at the Masquers Club in late 1978. With the honored woman at the dais, showing the audience a mounted movie poster of her as a child, was Pat Buttram.

From film to TV, everyone wanted Pat. *The New Misadventures of Ichabod Crane* was an animated television series, to be filmed in Canada, and they needed some well-known voices for it. Cast as the nag was Pat, and the nag's hound-dog partner was voiced by George Lindsey. These two voice actors were Disney favorites, so it pretty much guaranteed the success of this show. Kreskin gave gentle Ichabod Crane his voice, and Hazel Sherman breathed life into the jolly witch.

While dining at the Brown Derby one day, Pat was spotted by producer Caruth Byrd. Byrd asked his friend, Cotton Wittington, to introduce them. He did, and as the two men shook hands, Caruth was surprised when Pat said, "I've heard about you, Mr. Byrd." This was probably because Caruth had recently purchased the house next door to Gene Autry's.

The Byrd-Buttram association would prove quite fruitful in future years.

Pat was notified on January 14, 1979, that his brother Corry had died. Two bolts of lightning couldn't defeat him as a child, but now internal forces had. He was given a dialysis machine for his kidney problems and his wife Helen had learned how to use it at home, but it couldn't save him. He died of kidney failure.

The grief-stricken family knew that Pat and Hallie would want to be there, but there had been a bad storm in Alabama that week that made travel treacherous, so they advised their siblings to not even try to come. They felt it was better for them to miss the funeral than to risk a car accident on the way.

Nineteen-eighty began on a good note. Pat was elected Harlequin (president) of the Masquers Club. He enjoyed being the leader of this organization that meant so much to him. His friend Dale Berry says that when Pat first became its president, the club had been badly in debt. He was a good businessman, however, and a few dinners were all that was needed to make the club solvent again.

By autumn, however, Pat was experiencing a lull in his career. Being a sensitive man, it felt to him that he wasn't wanted or needed anymore. This troubled him greatly. Maybe the time was ripe for his retirement. After all, he was sixty-five. Maybe he should move back to Alabama and live out the rest of his life in anonymity.

Upon learning what was on Pat's mind, brother Gus went to work building a house for him there at Camp Maxwell. Pat sent most of his personal items to Alabama and gave away the rest; then he moved into the house that Gus built. The atmosphere in Haleyville is friendly, gentle, and warm. His family welcomed Pat back home with open arms. He asked his sister Hallie to come help him decorate the house, and she did so with joy. An entire wall of his living room was filled with photos, awards, and other memorabilia from his career. Prominently displayed here was the big, beautiful montage Hallie had made for him of his career.

This was a time of introspection for Pat. In an October 23, 1980 televised interview for the University of Alabama show *Uptown and Country*, funded in part by the Corporation for Public Broadcasting and taped from his new home, Pat was asked who his favorite comedian was. "The greatest of all time was Red Skelton. No one could touch him," he told producer/interviewer Charlotte Moakley. "Jackie Gleason can do sketches great, but he can't do a monolog. Bob Hope can do a monolog, but he's terrible in sketches. [Johnny] Carson does a great monolog; he can't do sketches. But Skelton can do it all."

Pat enjoyed telling this admiring young lady about his career. When asked about his *Green Acres* role, his eyes lit up. He said that he had patterned his Mr. Haney character after Colonel Tom Parker, whom he got to know while working with Elvis Presley. He felt that Parker was a country boy who could easily outsmart city folk, which was what Mr. Haney often did. Pat had been in three Presley films—*Roustabout, Wild in the Country*, and *Kissin' Cousins* -- but his parts were much diminished in most of them when later shown on television. What was Elvis Presley like, Moakley asked. "He was a delight, so polite," Pat responded. Presley even sent Pat's daughter photos and gifts, he said.

When the topic turned to the contrast between Hollywood and Haleyville, Pat said that Haleyville is an oxygen factory, compared to polluted Southern California. Alabama was a slow-paced place of first names and easy hellos. "I fit right in, just like I never left home," he told her. "I think every small-town boy leaves a little part of him back home in front of the drugstore."

He then treated Miss Moakley to a few of his newest one-liners:

"They've got a topless café here—a cyclone blew the roof off it."

"There's no place to go after 9:00 at night that you shouldn't go."

"The power plant here is a Die-Hard battery."

"The head of the mafia is a Phillipino."

Now, he was keeping busy giving lectures at colleges, conventions, and sales meetings. He liked personal appearances better than making movies or television shows, he said, because of the live audience. They provided instant feedback. He needed that to be sure that his act was working. Another reason he preferred performing live was because it warmed his heart every time he made his audience laugh. Their happiness was his happiness.

Pat's column now ran in hundreds of newspapers, and he was contemplating writing his autobiography. He realized that four generations had enjoyed his work. They might find his life story interesting, especially, he thought, his early days in Hollywood when he was living in the same hotel as people who later became legends—Errol Flynn, Doris Day, and Jackie Coogan. This would have been a magnificent book. It seems to have never been written, however.

"He was a cross-generation pollinator," says Chuck Southcott with a smile. "He does cross the generation lines. It's amazing that the young people who first find out about him catch his uniqueness. I see his appeal stick with the very young quickly."

➤   ➤

It didn't take long for Pat to realize that moving back to rural Alabama was a mistake. He had become so accustomed to the fast-paced Hollywood lifestyle that he felt antsy living in slow-moving Haleyville.

Too, being without him made Hollywood realize how much they needed him. They kept calling him back to emcee events, speak at dinners, appear on television shows, and lend his distinctive voice to animated projects. It was so nice to be needed again. Pretty soon, Pat decided unemployment wasn't for him after all and happily moved back to Los Angeles. That's where he felt he belonged.

"The great thing about Pat was that he had an amazing work ethic," says actor Randal Malone. "He loved to work. He was always busy. Even when he wasn't on a film project, he'd go to memorabilia shows and look for memorabilia about his wife."

He would later talk about someday retiring to the Motion Picture Home, but that would never happen. It wasn't meant to happen. As Kerry says, "Retirement would've killed him." As long as he was working and making people laugh, he was truly living.

Pat has entertained our highest-ranking officials. Seen here with President and Mrs. Ford. Note the mostly unamused Secret Service men in the background.
[From the collection of Kerry Galgano.]

With Nick Adams and Joey Heatherton in *Twilight of Honor*.
[From the collection of Kerry Galgano.]

Pat with the stars of *Green Acres*, Eddie Albert and Eva Gabor.

Most of Mr. Haney's scenes were with Mr. Douglas. [CBS publicity photo.]

"Could I interest you in this super-duper, gen-u-wine, deluxe radio?"

Pat with the show's hottest star, Arnold Ziffel. Pigs don't stay this small and cute forever, so they had quite a few porky actors playing this role over the years. [From the collection of Kerry Galgano.]

Pat socializing after-hours with Eva Gabor and her husband Richard Brown. [From the January, 1971, *TV Picture Life* magazine.]

With brother Gus, who was now unable to walk unassisted.
[From the collection of Gus and Rebecca Buttram.]

It's Pat Buttram Day! [From the collection of Hallie Reed.]

George Lindsey and Pat voiced their characters
together in the studio.

Pat's instantly recognizable characterization
on *Green Acres* [from the collection of Kerry
Galgano.]

Pat has worked with the greatest entertainers of his day. Seen here with Ed Wynn.
[From the collection of Kerry Galgano.]

A close-up of the montage that Hallie made for him, framed and hung on the wall.

This was taken immediately after the televised interview that took place in his "retirement home" in Haleyville, Alabama. Note the wall in the background, decorated by Hallie with memorabilia photos and awards from his very eventful career. [From the collection of Hallie Reed.]

Pat's good friend, Iron Eyes Cody. [From the collection of Kerry Galgano.]

Some very prominent people show up at these Golden Boot Awards ceremonies: John Wayne and Ben Johnson. [From the collection of Kerry Galgano.]

James Stewart receiving his Golden Boot Award from Gene Autry. [From the collection of Kerry Galgano.]

Chapter Eleven

Gus **was surprised** to receive a letter from actor Karl Malden. It said:

Rev. Gus Buttram:

Your brother was kind enough to do me a great favor and I would like you to accept this small check as a thank you.

I can only say good luck and I'm a better man knowing Pat.

Sincerely,
Karl Malden

What was that all about? No one will say, but the check was very much appreciated.

It was about this time that Pat discovered a new employee in the Autry office, which was located at 5858 Sunset Boulevard. Maxine Hansen was originally hired as the assistant to Gene's assistant. When her superior passed away in 1985, Maxine was promoted to her position; when Gene passed on, she became Mrs. Autry's assistant. She's still working in that office to this day and has many very fond memories of Pat. "He was part of the office because I feel that he and Mr. Autry were as close as any brothers could be," she says. "He and Mr. Autry were so close. When I would answer the phone, it would either be Mr. Autry going, 'Well, where's Patrick?" or Pat going, "Where is he? I'm supposed to go to breakfast with him." The two men were spiritual soulmates, she feels.

On July 19, 1981, Pat was one of two witnesses at the small wedding of Gene Autry and Jacqueline Ellam. Gene's first wife, Ina, had died the previous year.

Jackie Autry recalls, "When Gene and I got married in July of 1981, he first called another dear friend, Johnny Grant, and asked him if he could find a preacher to marry us. Once he determined that one was available on a Sunday (of all days) he immediately called Pat and asked Pat if he would come and join us and be our second witness. I think he wanted his two best friends there, not only to be our witnesses, but also to share his joy in this very special occasion.

"For many years we used to kid about which of the two of them was the flower girl and which was the ring bearer.

"Prior to the actual wedding, the four of us met at Lakeside Country Club for breakfast. Pat, with his usual sense of humor, said, 'Jackie, I have a gift for you, and since you need something new, I want you to have this diamond pin.' Upon opening it, I found a dime welded to a chrome safety pin. He then went on to say, 'and you need something borrowed,' so he gave me his handkerchief. My wedding dress was blue...When he got to the 'old' part, he stated that he didn't need to give me anything old, because I was marrying it." So Pat was satisfied that the bride now had the traditional "Something old, something new, something borrowed, something blue."

Once the ceremony was completed, it was time to face the media. At such times, Pat could be serious. "It's always a sign of a good marriage when a man marries a short time after his wife dies," Pat told reporter George Hunter. "It shows he wants to recapture the happiness he knew as a married man." Pat knew that his friend had been missing Ina so much and needed someone with whom to share the rest of his life. "Jackie has made him very happy. She's a very smart businesswoman, too, which gives them something extra in common."

⇾   ⇽

Soon afterward, Pat was cast in the Walt Disney animated movie *The Fox and the Hound*. "He was in five Disney movies, which is unusual," sister Hallie says. "He loved doing them because they would have him read like an old hound dog and they watched him, and I can just see him when I see that movie—that dog—he has Pat's expression." Yes, Pat acknowledged the fact that Chief, the dog, has his eyebrows and nose. "I've got a nose that qualifies me for handicapped parking," he joked to *The Tampa Tribune* reporter Greg Tozian.

Nevertheless, this film had its audience—both adults and children—in tears. It deals with a relationship between a puppy (voiced by Corey Feldman in the early sequences and Kurt Russell later) and a baby fox (with the voices of Keith Mitchell and Mickey Rooney). They are the best of friends, thinking they always will be, but others step in to change all that. Other luminaries who lent their voices for this animated film were Pearl Bailey (as the wise owl), Jack Albertson (as the grouchy hunter), Jeanette Nolan (as the kindhearted Widow Tweed), Sandy Duncan (as a lovely lady fox), John Fiedler (as a hospitable porcupine), and John McIntire (as the very unhospitable badger). This film incorporated beautiful, soft pastel scenery with high drama and occasional comic relief by the birds' determination to get a caterpillar. Pat's character, the old hunting dog, also provides some of the comedy as he makes a bid for sympathy after being injured. None was forthcoming, however, because his owner was the crusty old hunter. Pearl Bailey warmly sang the story's beautiful songs. Like all Disney animated films, the makers took a great deal of time to provide us with a quality product.

It was in this year, too, that Pat was chosen to play Tad Miller, a small-town fun-house owner in the *Darkroom* episode, "The Partnership." Narrated by James Coburn, this was a spooky story in which Pat's character turned out just the opposite of what one would expect.

It must have been around this time that Pat interviewed stuntman extraordinaire Yakima Canutt and Cherokee actor Iron Eyes Cody on camera about their careers. The conversation with the former touched on the subject of stunts that went wrong, causing injury to the actors. As tempted as Pat must have been to talk about such an accident that nearly cost him his own life back in 1951, he didn't. Instead, he was focused completely on the man he was questioning. These interviews were included with eleven movies on the three-DVD set, *Cowboy Heroes of the Silver Screen*, compiled in 2004.

⇉ ⇇

At the Reagans' invitation, Pat was visiting their ranch during the 1980s. Edward Asner was the president of the Screen Actors Guild at that time, a position that the President had held a couple of decades earlier. President Reagan asked Pat what he thought of Ed Asner, who was left-leaning in his politics while Reagan was, of course, right-leaning. Pat re-assured Reagan, "Don't worry about it, Mr. President. Asner is just an actor." The halls must have echoed with laughter at that quip!

Pat would often write material for his friends. One bit he gave to President Reagan was "A recession is when your neighbor loses his job. A depression is when you lose yours." It was a pleasure to give him one-liners regularly because Reagan had such a fine delivery. Many notes of acknowledgment from Reagan resulted. Here is one that was dated May 25, 1983, on White House stationery:

Dear Pat:

Just a note to let you know how grateful I am for your as-sistance. I have a fine, competent speechwriting staff and they do a great job in putting together some very erudite material. However, sometimes it takes a special touch of an old pro to add the sparkle that keeps the audience from snoozing off! Thanks to you, some of my speeches have found a very attentive audi-ence.

Nancy joins me in sending our warmest regards.

Sincerely,
Ron

Then Pat was given a good role in another movie, *Choices*, which was also released this year. Based on a true story, John Carluccio is both a star football player and a prodigal violinist. He loves both endeavors equally. However, he is suddenly disqualified from sports by the team's doctor be-cause of his hearing impairment, in spite of the fact that John's hearing aid enables him to hear normally. This is a very inspiring film in which Paul Carafotes played John beautifully, Victor French was his father, and Val Avery was his coach. Pat's character, Pops, is the proprietor of an es-tablishment in which rough teens hang out. It is an unsavory place for John, and Pops advises him to stay away from it and to devote his time to perfecting his music. Good, solid advice from a caring man. Even though John joins the wrong crowd for a while and acts out his frustration in very unwise ways, he finally comes out on top, thanks to his inner strength and all the brave people in his life who fight his biggest foe—prejudice.

Pat still made regular visits to the Autry office. "He was a flirt, but it was just a harmless flirt," said Maxine. "I think he was very lonely [after Sheila died]." Even though he missed Sheila terribly, he had a "the show must go on" way about him, channeling his affections into lighthearted hugs and kisses to the Autry staff.

It was getting close to Christmas, so he took Maxine and two of the other ladies in the office to lunch. Once they were seated at the restaurant, he presented each of them with a gift. "I remember mine so well," she said. "It's a hand-held egg beater, but this was a *tiny* little baby one. I still have it. I love it. It's a tiny thing that if you made an egg and want to scramble it, you can just put this little thing in." Maxine loved his thoughtfulness. Another time, perhaps for Secretary's Day, he gave her a very special book. "It's a rare book about English places and the countryside. He seemed to understand what would be enjoyed by a particular person. He was very, very generous that way."

During that lunch, the inevitable excited fans approached the table. "He was totally okay with it. Totally. It's like he didn't invite it, but he didn't throw it away. The same with Mr. Autry. He really was very respectful to people."

Having lunch regularly with Gene was a given in Pat's life. Jackie Autry recalls, "They looked out for each other and I used to chuckle when the two of them took off for lunch every week together. The reason for my amusement was Pat was blind in one eye and Gene was blind in another. When Pat would come to a stop sign, he would ask if it was OK to pull out. Gene, of course, would be looking to his right since he was sitting in the passenger seat and tell him it was OK. Unfortunately, Gene's right eye was the one that had no vision, so I often wondered how he knew it was OK to make a left turn onto a street when Gene didn't have the foggiest notion on what was or was not coming."

Mrs. Autry continues, "Pat also knew that Gene was unable to drive anymore, so he went out of his way to come to the house and pick up Gene when they decided it was time to get together and rehash the same old stories. But watching the two of them together and listening to them giggle like little school boys was a lot of fun."

Back at home and thereabouts, Pat was able to combine two things he loved. Kerry was now a married lady with a child. Pat was quite fond of taking photographs and just adored his granddaughter, Natalie. Therefore, his siblings would receive many snapshots of little Natalie in the mail.

He also liked to tease his niece Mary. Once, he bought her a beautiful painting, but wrapped it up as a gift for her husband "Dos." Her resulting confusion made him laugh. In honor of her profession, he also got Mary a "Love a nurse" mug.

Chapter Twelve

The Golden Boot Awards

Pat wanted very much to publicly recognize the hard-working people who had made the Western genre so successful. The stars were a big part of this success, but so were the writers, stunt people, directors, and character actors. They should be rewarded, too, he felt. Actor Bob Steele was uppermost in Pat's mind at this point. Honoring Steele was something in his power to do, now that he was a top officer of the Masquer's Club.

He began making his plans and everything fell right into place. Here's a letter he wrote in September to actor Clayton Moore, known to many as television's Lone Ranger:

Dear Clayton:

As Harlequin of the Masquers Club, the Oldest Actors Club in Hollywood, we are happy to invite you to the "Greatest Round Up of Western Stars in History".

On November 20, 1982 at our Club-house we are honoring the Fightenest, Scrappiest, Cowboy of them all, BOB STEELE.

Bob has asked that you sit on the Dais with him on this big evening along with Burt Reynolds, Iron Eyes Cody, Gene Autry, Randolph Scott, Charles Starrett and many many more. It will be a night that will go down in Hollywood History as The Last Great Round Up of Western Stars.

Let me know as soon as possible and we will give you more details.

Moore accepted this invitation and sat with Steele on the dais while his wife sat at Pat's table. The award presented by emcee Pat to the guest of honor was a fancy belt buckle with the image of a golden boot on it. Applauding this presentation were also Roy Rogers, Dale Evans, and Larry Storch. It was a gala event.

Once the party was over and most of the attendees had departed, the remaining men—Pat, Bob Campbell, Caruth Byrd, and Ray Webb—went to the Masquers Club bar downstairs and made plans. Pat stressed the importance of getting these Western-genre people together regularly to eat, drink, and swap stories. They deserved to hear applause again and loved to be with others who participated in that glorious era. "Westerns will always live in my heart and pay no rent," Pat would say.

The others agreed with his ideas and decided to hold an event annually, calling it the Golden Boot Awards. It would serve a dual purpose: To honor the awards' recipients, and to raise funds for the Motion Picture & Television Fund's retirement, childcare, health and human services programs. Their hospital had taken good care of Sheila during her illness, so Pat was happy that the Golden Boots would benefit this worthy organization.

Making up for lost time, twenty-four people were honored at the first official Golden Boot Awards in 1983. They were Bruce Boxleitner, Charles Starrett, Clayton Moore, Dale Evans, Dick Alexander, Al Wyatt, Ben Johnson, Bob Steele, Doug McClure, Eddie Dean, Forrest Tucker, Gene Autry, Jack Elam, Lash LeRue, Lee Majors, Lee Van Cleef, Linda Stirling, Monte Hale, Nat Levine, Rex Allen, Roy Rogers, Slim Pickens, and Sunset Carson, with the In Memorial Award going to Will Rogers.

In a turn of events, the Golden Boot committee voted to present one of the 1984 awards to Pat. They had wanted to do that the first year, but Pat did not feel that it would be right. Now, in the second year, he relented. He had long patted his fellow laborers on the back for their work in Westerns, and now the committee felt that it was time for a tribute to go to him.

The Golden Boot Awards grew by leaps and bounds. According to Caruth Byrd, profits given so far to the MPTF have totaled about $300,000-$400,000. "[Pat] really cared about his charity work for us and raising as much money as he could," says MPTF representative Marcia Braunstein. Pat's sparkling wit was usually the highlight of Golden Boot Award presentations over the years.

By the 2000s, the event would be held in the large ballroom of the Beverly Hilton Hotel. "There are hundreds of tables because they pull between five hundred and seven hundred people. It's jam-packed!" says

Donna Martell, who received this honor in 2002 and has her trophy prominently displayed in the center of her family room's wall unit. The award is now a golden boot atop a hardwood base, with a brass plate on which is engraved the recipient's name and achievements.

Harry Carey, Jr., who was given the award himself, recalls its founder. "That was his dream, to reward the best Western actors," he says. "It's kind of gotten out of control now, but the first ten years of it were wonderful."

"What a wonderful thing that he put together for these people who work all of their lives. To accomplish and to receive a Boot is probably the crème-de-la-crème," Donna Martell says. "They're still together, still going strong, and still making a lot of people very happy."

Chapter Thirteen

Caruth Byrd had been given a fancy "a cowboy car" by his friend Chill Wills, who was dying of cancer. Not needing a car himself, Caruth then decided what to do with it. He had produced a film called *Lone Star Country*, and asked Pat to come entertain at the production's wrap party. Pat agreed, and did a wonderful presentation. Caruth then came onstage and handed him the title and keys to that car, saying this was for the home for wayward children that Pat was involved in. "That's the only time I ever saw Pat Buttram not say anything," Caruth says. "He didn't say a dadgum thing. Had tears in his eyes and walked off the stage." The grand gesture had touched Pat deeply.

It was around this time that Pat's path crossed that of fan Larry Given. Says Larry, "During the 1980s I was working on completing a signed group photo of the main characters in *Green Acres*. Both Eddie Albert and Eva Gabor had already signed my cast photo. When Mr. Buttram finished signing the photo, he sent it back to me with an extremely nice letter. I had previously shared my thoughts with him concerning his career in Westerns. After obtaining Mr. Buttram's autograph on the *Green Acres* cast photo, he would go on to write me several more times. One could tell in his letters that he dearly loved his fans."

The man, in fact, seemed to care about everyone. Says entertainment executive Earl Blair, "I found him to be genuine and very savvy…sort of a clearing house of information on what was going on in the biz. He knew just about everything about everyone. I saw him work as toastmaster for several banquets, including a Masquers dinner and the first Golden Boot. He had an incredible wit and was far funnier as a stand-up or host than the buffoonish bumpkin he played in the Autry films. As with most clowns, he understood the human condition and had far greater depth than the shallowness of a smile or laughter's soon forgotten echo."

Actor Randal Malone agrees. "I was always so impressed that Hollywood never changed him. He became a star, had a very successful career, but he remained a very earnest and loyal person to everyone who knew him. He was so loved." Malone continues, "You never saw Pat when he wasn't smiling. You never saw Pat when he didn't have something good to say about somebody. Even if they weren't the greatest, you never heard him say one disparaging remark about them."

Jackie Autry, too, noticed Pat's empathy for others. "Pat was down to earth," she says, "and although he had financial difficulties from time to time (primarily because he did not save money for his retirement), he nevertheless always had time for others. In this regard, at one point Gene put Pat on his personal payroll just to make sure he had enough money to carry him from month to month. Pat, not wanting to feel like he was taking money he did not earn, would go out and represent Gene at a variety of functions that Gene could not make."

➳   ⏺

Not only was Pat working on the west coast, but he also made himself available for speaking engagements throughout the country. He is listed in the Midwest Program Service Inc.'s 1982 directory, which contains 187 platform speakers, lecturers and entertainers. He was in good company. Also represented by this service were Paul Harvey, David Brinkley, Ann Landers, and Curt Gowdy.

He even leant his talents to General Motors, in their motivational video for their parts-department staff called "Parts Smart: Come Dressed and Ready to Play." In it, he played the part of two men, the host and the parts-department employee. Knowing his history, we would realize that this was made after Pat had lost the small finger of his left hand. Because he showed no self-consciousness about it at all, however, one wouldn't notice it unless he was looking for it.

➳   ⏺

In the late summer of 1983, it appeared that romance had re-entered Pat's life. Her name was Gloris Slattery, and she was the general manager of the Greater Los Angeles Press Club. "Gloris is a beautiful, intelligent woman and I love her with all my heart," he told *The National Enquirer* that September. They were making wedding plans.

By Thanksgiving, however, they began rethinking this. "I guess I got cold feet," he said. "We both felt it wasn't exactly the right thing." She began dating others.

Pat's health was again becoming an issue early in 1984. He underwent heart bypass surgery in February to mend what had become flawed so he could get on with his life. While still in the hospital recovering from surgery, Pat got word from a visiting friend that Gloris had married 52-year-old sound man George Bonnell, reported the May 15th *National Enquirer.* "I have tossed and turned through sleepless nights, wondering if I could have done anything to make things turn out differently," they quoted him as saying in this exclusive interview. "In the darkness I've shed a few tears over the loss of a beautiful relationship. I still love her, but I'm a survivor. Life goes on."

Later, as was his nature, he would joke about it. "When people ask me what happened to our engagement, I have a stock joke. I say, 'Well, she got married to some other guy and after that we just drifted apart.'" In all honesty, though, he accepted the fact that it didn't work out. "I'll just look back on it as a beautiful memory," he said. "Pat Buttram will live and love again!"

❧   ☙

At a January 1985 awards luncheon of the Oregon Horticultural Society, Pat was the featured speaker. *The Oregonian* reporter Julie Tripp liked best the joke he told about President Reagan: "He went from the broadcast booth to the White House, which could scare you to death when you think about where Howard Cosell might end up."

Later that year, his KGBS friend Bob Morgan helped him put Channel 64 KVVT on the air in Victorville. His partners would be Ray Webb and Riley Jackson—Webb did the set-up work with the FCC, Jackson was the financial backer, and Pat did the promotional work. Since then, the station has changed its call letters to KHIZ, but is still channel 64.

Good friend Ray Webb was, in fact, Pat's most frequent breakfast companion. Their favorite morning place was the Sportsmen's Lodge Coffee Shop, where Gene Autry and Monte Hale would often join them.

Pat had come up with a line that has often been repeated by others. It's one of Johnny Western's favorites, about Gene's extreme business success. Western says. "It's rumored that by the time Gene passed away, he was worth $600 million." Pat's response to such talk was, "Gene Autry used to ride off into the sunset. Now, he owns it."

⇥   ⇤

The Golden Boot Awards had really caught on. Pat noticed that the people involved would come to town from all over the country the day before the event, but had nothing in particular to do that evening. He asked his friend Jim Roberts to help. Happy to oblige his friend, Roberts held a roundup party, complete with buffalo burgers, the night before the award ceremony. This party would become a joyous tradition in the ensuing years. One year, it was reported by (L.A.) *Daily News* columnist Dennis McCarthy on a Friday in August in this humorous way:

> The bad guys started driftin' into town about high noon Thursday.
>
> Jim Roberts, Ben Cooper, and Jack Iverson were seen tying up their SUVs in the parking lot behind the Sportsmen's Lodge in Studio City.
>
> Behind them came black hats Jon Locke, Mike Forest, Morgan Woodard and dozens of other old TV and movie cowboys who spent long careers biting the dust for a living.
>
> A few of the good guys who shot them were there, too, but not many. Dale Robertson, star of TV's "Tales of Wells Fargo," which ran from 1957 to 1962, got into town a few hours ahead of Roy Rogers' old singing group, the Sons of the Pioneers.
>
> The present group of Pioneers are in town to receive the prestigious Golden Boot award Saturday night. It's the equivalent of the Oscar for Western movies, and the Pioneers are getting the first Golden Boot ever awarded for music.
>
> It's a big, classy event at the Beverly Hilton and will benefit the Motion Picture Country Home and Hospital in Woodland Hills, so the bad guys have to be on their best behavior.
>
> But that won't be the case tonight over at the Sportsmen's Lodge, where they'll be blowing off steam at the annual Jim Roberts Roundup.
>
> "This is where the fun starts," said bad guy Locke, who spent a career being killed by just about every good guy on TV.

Pat was given a wonderful opportunity in 1987. Would he team up with his buddy Gene Autry to introduce the modern-day audience to the Western movies of yore in a TNN series? Why, sure he would! This series, *Melody Ranch Theater*, first aired on April 6, 1987 and ran for almost two years. Gene and Pat hosted the show, discussed some of the behind-the-scenes goings-on of that week's movie, then ran the fine old film. The two would appear and talk a bit at breaks in the movie, as well. From the closing credits, we learn that Pat was the show's researcher and one of its writers. Gene trusted him, and Pat delivered.

The sight of Pat and Gene sitting together and talking about the old days was a very familiar one to Johnny Western. "Gene just loved to reminisce," he says. "After he became Mr. Businessman, he wasn't rubbing elbows with a lot of showbiz people anymore and he missed it. Not to the point of doing them again, especially after he had the stroke. It was impossible for him to do those things. So the reminiscing became a huge part, and Pat was absolutely there for him every step of the way. He treasured that."

In the episode in which the spotlight was on their 1950 film *Indian Territory*, Pat and Gene revealed a secret behind some of the fight scenes. When Gene and the "bad guy" were fighting in a river, it often wasn't going as smoothly as it looked. He was still wearing his heavy cowboy boots, gun and holster, etc., which made it difficult to keep his balance on the slippery river bottom. Sometimes, while it appeared to us that they were fighting, what they were really doing was keeping each other upright. Pat declared that it was much easier to do such a fight scene with a stuntman than with another actor because stuntmen were much more experienced and knowledgeable about those things.

➳   ⤞

Pat was awarded a star on the Hollywood Walk of Fame in August 1988. Located at 6382 Hollywood Boulevard, it is an acknowledgment of the great success that he had achieved in the world of television. Among his friends attending the ceremony was Gene Autry, of course, and also Lash LaRue, Iron Eyes Cody, Eddie Albert, George Gobel, and Denver Pyle. The very next year, Alabama would honor Pat in a similar way—with a star on the Alabama Walk of Fame, which was located on the sidewalk of the Alabama Theater on Third Avenue in Birmingham. "My dad was a minister up in North Alabama," Pat responded, "and he always said if I stayed in show business I would wind up on the street, so that's where I am."

On February 4, 1989, the 1950s Western star Rex Allen wanted to open a Western museum and movie house in Willcox, Arizona. Would his friends help? You bet! Roy Rogers, Gene Autry, Pedro Gonzales, and Pat joined with him in a fundraiser dinner and celebrity roast.

It was around this time, too, that brother Gus and his wife Becky received money from Pat. They were to use it to take their German exchange student and his friends to Disney World and Epcott Center during their spring break. Pat's thoughtfulness, as well as Gus and Becky's loving hospitality, would make this a very memorable time in the young man's life.

Pat's family was so proud of him. Gus and Becky established the Pat Buttram Museum in downtown Haleyville, Alabama. Its walls were covered with lumber taken from the parsonage in which Pat was born. Pat was a major contributor to this museum, gifting it with such things as his "Mr. Haney" clothes, items from the back of Haney's wagon, and a Gene Autry-signed saddle. Inside the museum was "Mr. Haney's Trading Post." Pat isn't the only one honored in this museum. Also on display is the red telephone that was used to make the very first 9-1-1 call in the nation. This emergency system originated in Haleyville.

He was still getting together with buddy Gene Autry on a regular basis. Gene, now owner of the California Angels baseball team, would often be seen sitting with Pat at the games.

And there was yet another reason to smile. Daughter Kerry had given birth to her second child, baby Angie. A doting grandpa was Pat, for sure.

And there was, of course, his work.

Buttram was chosen to appear in the third installment of the hit *Back to the Future* series. This one had an old-west theme and Pat was seen with two other popular "old timers"—Dub Taylor and Harry Carey, Jr. - sitting at a table in the barroom at various times throughout the story. In the trio's final scene, suspense was high. Marty McFly (Michael J. Fox) who, for this time-travel trip, goes by the name Clint Eastwood, is committed to meet with the show's villain, Mad Dog Tannen (Thomas F. Wilson), in a duel at eight o'clock, while Doc (Christopher Lloyd) is unconscious in the bar. It was now that time, and Tannen is waiting outside for him. Knowing that gunslinging isn't his forte, McFly hesitates. That's when Buttram's character has one of the funniest lines in the movie: "You'd better face up to it, son, 'cause…[if you don't] everybody, everywhere will say Clint Eastwood is the biggest yellow-belly in the West." This eagerly-anticipated movie was released in 1990.

"It was fun," Harry Carey, Jr., says. "All we had to do was sit around the table in the saloon." These veteran actors had a great time doing the film.

It would be the last time the two men worked together.

≫   ≪

In addition to handing out their own awards, the Golden Boot Award presentations were now also bestowing the Hollywood Westerner Hall of Fame "President Reagan Award." Big names from near and far attended the event, or to participate in it. At the Seventh Annual Golden Boot Awards event, held at the Los Angeles Registry Hotel on August 5, 1989, this was the agenda:

Introduction .... Roger Davis
Invocation .... Iron Eyes Cody
Celebrity Introduction ...... Rob Word

DINNER

Master of Ceremonies .... Pat Buttram
Music .... Boot Straps
Auction .... Denver Pyle

GOLD BOOT AWARDS

HONOREES	PRESENTERS
John Ireland	Jane Russell
Johnny Cash	Gene Autry
Angie Dickinson	Earl Holliman
Robert Fuller	Clayton Moore
Dick Jones	Jock Mahoney
Ellen Corby	Ann Doran
Paul Malvern	Hank Worden
Casey Tibbs	Ben Johnson & Richard Farnsworth
Robert Duvall	James Stewart
Andy Devine	Guy Madison & Roy Rogers

HOLLYWOOD WESTERNER HALL OF FAME
"PRESIDENT REAGAN AWARD" TO
JAMES STEWART

The auction incorporated into the gala event was to further benefit the Golden Boot's favorite cause, the Motion Picture and Television Country House and Hospital. Among items donated for this auction was a set of two Colt commemorative .45 guns, Jack Holt's polo boots, original scripts from *Hondo* and *Giant*, a Stetson hat, Cavalry saddle, and Bruce Boxleitner's hat.

Being dedicated to the Western genre, the glossy forty-five-page program handed out to the Awards' attendees included a page entitled "Republic's Western Street." It contained six beautiful photographs of the old-time town on the back lot at Republic—all very familiar to Western actors and their fans. At the bottom of the page is the note: "Pictures were taken by Pat Buttram one week before it was razed."

"Pat was instrumental in getting my Golden Boot," says Robert Fuller. "People paid a lot of money to go to the Golden Boot just to see him [Pat] emcee it."

✎   ✎

Around this time, Pat was invited to Haleyville, Alabama, to help them celebrate Chitlin' Day. He gladly obliged. During the event, the photographer wanted a picture of Pat eating one of their delicacies. Chitlins, more properly referred to as chitterlings, are made of the same thing that sausage casings are. Pat could handle that, but the chitlins he was given were cold and not at all appetizing. Nevertheless, he used his best acting skill and smiled for the camera as he ate.

May of 1990 promised a real treat to *Green Acres* fans. A reunion show, the TV movie *Return to Green Acres*, would bring most of the regulars together again—Pat, Eddie Albert, Eva Gabor, Tom Lester, Frank Cady, Sid Melton, Mary Grace Canfield, and Alvy Moore. On the day it aired, though, many fans were disappointed. It was wonderful to see the cast together again, but the storyline didn't work. The writer/creator of the original series, Jay Sommers, was deceased, and it appeared that this production was written by people who did not fully understand the personalities of the original characters.

Pat's Pearl of Wisdom

"Why is it that the people who own three-quarters of the oil in the world ride camels?"

"It's not the duty of a toastmaster to bore the audience, but to introduce those who will."

This Buttramism was recalled by Wink Martindale: "Like the Mississippi River, the older we get, the harder it gets to hold our water."

"You know you are getting old when someone compliments you on your alligator shoes and you are barefoot."

"Every family should have three children. If one turns out to be a genius, the other two can support him."

"The only thing that comes to the folks who wait is kidney trouble."

He always has time to give an autograph to a fan. Shown here in Victorville.
[From the collection of Kerry Galgano—Daily Press.]

When Pat was the speaker, no one could keep a straight face.
Seen here with President and Mrs. Reagan on his right and John
Wayne on his left. [From the collection of Hallie Reed.]

Above: Pat's dear friend Richard Farnsworth. Left: and Richard Farnsworth again, this time with Denver Pyle. [From the collection of Kerry Galgano.]

With Esther Williams and Steve Allen.
[From the collection of Kerry Galgano.]

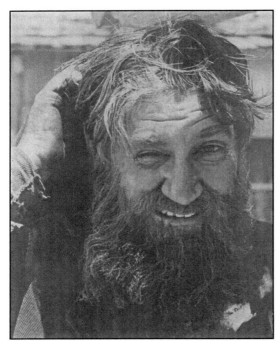

In *Pistols 'n' Petticoats*
"The Golden Fleece."

How many of these great Western stars can you name?
[From the collection of Kerry Galgano.]

His best friends were there to honor Pat when he received his star on the Hollywood Walk of Fame.
[From the collection of Hallie Reed, courtesy of Zella Fuller.]

A close-up of his Hollywood star. [From the collection of Hallie Reed.]

A close-up of Pat's star on the Alabama Walk of Fame.

Pat with fellow "old timer," Dub Taylor, celebrating the release of Back to the Future, Part III. Some feel this was the best installment of the 3-movie series.

Being interviewed with Bob Hope. [from the collection of Kerry Galgano— photo by Traude.]

Pat was much more experienced at this than the other radio personalities were. [Courtesy of Gene Autry Entertainment.]

Making an appearance with Vincent Price.
[From the collection of Kerry Galgano.]

Pat did indeed live and love again. Here, he's enjoying a lighthearted moment with his friend Suzanne Spaun. (Photo by Traude)

Good-naturedly going along with the gunplay of grandnephews Walden and Candler at the Gene Autry Museum. [From the collection of Zella Fuller.]

His funeral took place at Maxwell Chapel, the church his mother's family had founded before he was born.

Beside the chapel is the graveyard. His tombstone says: "A man deserves paradise who can make his companions laugh."

The Golden Boot Awards in 1994 honored Pat's lifetime of laughter. [Cover artist Ivan Jesse Curtis.]

Kerry's favorite picture of her dad.

Chapter Fourteen

Pat would call his oldest sister Peggy twice a week and they would have long, leisurely conversations. "We'd have some of the most wonderful talks," she told *Times Daily* reporter Terry Pace. "He'd fill me in on all the Hollywood gossip, and we'd talk about politics and everything under the sun."

Chuck Southcott was later to become the program director of Autry-owned radio station KMPC in Los Angeles. Here's how he tells of his discovery of Pat Buttram's extraordinary talent: "The program director, my boss, was the general manager of the radio station and the president of Golden West Broadcasters. His name was Bill Ward. We'd go to lunch quite often and I'd said, 'You know, Bill, I heard Pat with Mark and Brian (that's a rock 'n' roll comedy team on radio in Los Angeles).' 'I'm a fan of Pat's, but he ripped those guys apart with comedy!' He was hipper than those two young rock 'n' roll guys, who thought they were having fun with the old man, and the old man just *took care of it*. I couldn't believe it. He was so funny and so much hipper than those young guys. I said, 'We've got to use him in the morning. I don't care where we put him, KMPC or the rock station.'" Ward decided to add Buttram to Robert W. Morgan's *Music of Your Life* show. "Within a week, he was on the air." And on the air he remained from 1986 through 1992. "I think it added some to his life, I really do," continues Southcott. "He came in every day. Robert didn't like the idea because he was the top guy in the city for many years, and he balked a little bit in the beginning. But about a month after it started, he loved Buttram. He thought he was just great. They got along really well, and they worked very well together."

155

KMPC was a major Los Angeles station. "That was the station that all the radio people wanted to work for because Autry was a legendary boss. He was known as a very good employer and an excellent broadcaster," says Southcott. "He did an hour in the morning with Robert W. He was only hired really to do a five-minute piece at 8:35 every weekday morning, but he came in at 8:00 and just sat there with Robert until 9:00. He'd throw in his lines and Robert would put his guest mike on, then he'd do his piece at 8:35. It was sponsored. The rest of the time, Pat was ready to talk about the news or anything. That was the highest-rated hour of the radio station. It was really amazing. Gene Autry was asked one time about his listening habits and he said, 'I never miss Pat.' He listened every day and they ate lunch together just about every day at a specific place in the San Fernando Valley."

In addition to the regular show, Pat also took part in some of the radio dramas aired over KMPC from the Gene Autry Museum in Los Angeles (now named the Museum of the American West). The museum had a theater that seated about two hundred fifty people. "We're really a music station," says Southcott, "but once a month, usually on a Sunday night, we'd have this [radio drama] and we'd repeat it a second time. I think it was the second one we aired. We'd charge admission and the money would go to the museum." He continues, "Quite often, Pat was part of the radio dramas. They were primarily westerns, complete with both a sound-effects man in the booth and a live, on-stage sound-effects man. Quite a few of the broadcasts featured Pat in one of the roles."

Pat was fond of Chuck. "One day he brought me one of those old lobby sheets. They look like posters, but they're frame-able size. He brought me one with Gene Autry, and his late wife Sheila Ryan was in it. It's a picture of him on the floor with suds all over him. He got Autry to sign it, he signed it, and he even signed it for his late wife, saying, 'This is from Sheila, too.' I treasure that."

The calendar might have been telling Pat that it was time to retire, but to do so would be against his nature. He always shared his humor whenever and wherever he could. Chuck Southcott is also an on-air talent, and all he had to do was say something like, "Pat, I have to introduce Ray Anthony," and Pat would provide him with three jokes that always worked. Well, *almost* always. "The only time I blew it," Chuck says, "was when Pat was in the audience…He made me nervous. He was the only one who did."

Southcott returned the favor by driving Pat where he wanted to go at night. "Pat couldn't or wouldn't or didn't like to drive at night the last few years. I don't know which it was—couldn't, wouldn't, or didn't want to—but whenever there was a nighttime event and we were both involved, I'd pick him up and take him…Some sort of a vision thing, he said, with nighttime driving in his later years."

"[KMPC] was our flagship station," says Maxine Hansen from the Autry office. "After he finished the show, he'd come upstairs. I found him to be a very funny man, but I also found him to be a very sensitive and intelligent man." Maxine was in awe of these qualities. "He wrote this incredible poem about where the cowboys have gone. It's just incredible," she says. "It shows totally the sensitivity of this man—that beneath that joking exterior and one-liners was this incredible writer. He was a very thoughtful, very sensitive man."

Karla Buhman worked in the Autry promotions department, so she got to know Pat, too. "I first got to know him as the sharpest, wittiest man in Hollywood," she says. "It always impressed me that his jokes and comments on the contemporary things happening in the media or the news, whatever was the popular subject at the time, were the wittiest." He would also spend some time visiting with Karla after the shows. "I really grew to cherish these," she says. "What also impressed me, and I found this true, too, with Gene Autry, that you watch all the movie and TV shows, and listen to the radio shows, and they have this really fun personality. When I would sit and visit with Pat, that same personality was there! The friendship and camaraderie of Gene and Pat, you can see in films like *Mule Train*. You can see just how they respond to each other and you see that smile on Gene like, 'That's Pat doing his thing.' That friendship is so powerful and so meaningful."

One morning, Karla had an assignment that stands out in her mind as a special memory of Pat. "One of the jobs I had to do in the promotion department was work with all the radio personalities and have their portraits taken for publicity, newspapers, and different things. We had all these big hotshot A.M. radio DJs and all these big hotshot F. M. radio DJs, and Pat. I spent the whole morning with our photographer, doing these portrait shots dealing with these radio personalities. Then comes Pat. He's an older man. He comes in and the photographer says, 'Okay. Let's go.' At that moment, Pat just *lit* up, held his hat at the perfect tilt, had his hand at the perfect height, he was *so* poised instantly. Every single shot the photographer took was perfect. And I'd spent the whole day with these other Los Angeles radio personalities, who couldn't have their picture taken. It was difficult to get them to have their picture taken. Then here this older gentleman comes in and just glows. I said, 'Pat! How did you *do* that?'

He just said, 'Well, I've been doing it for years.' It just so impressed me that moment, his professionalism. I have yet to see a contemporary entertainer in my first-hand experience with that knowledge and power that Pat had. It was just a neat moment for me."

➳ ❦

It was around the Christmastime of 1990 that Pat was diagnosed with throat cancer. This cancer is usually associated with heavy smoking, but that was not the case with Pat. He had never been a smoker. He took time off from his radio work to deal with this disease. He had surgery and endured seven weeks of twice-a-day radiation treatments. The recuperation period was painful, but Pat refused to take painkillers for fear of becoming addicted. After the treatment, it took a few more weeks for his voice to return. Once it did, he wanted to work, but had not regained his strength yet. KMPC to the rescue. They brought a microphone to his den so he could do his spot from home. It took a mighty effort for him to enunciate as clearly as he used to, but he did it. The equipment and engineering were top quality, making it sound as if Pat were in the studio along with the rest of the performers.

Pat was no longer living at the house he and Sheila had furnished together. Rather, he sold the house and now had an apartment at the Horace Heidt Estates in Sherman Oaks. This was a small one-story community of showbiz folk. "He had quite a lovely home there," says Chuck Southcott. "It was a very active location and he seemed pretty happy there." It was from this apartment that Pat phoned his old friend Donna Martell. During that conversation, he told her how pleased he was with his life's accomplishments. "He was very proud of the fact that he had really made something of himself," she recalls. "He was such a sweet, down-to-earth man."

➳ ❦

It was a special occasion for brother Gus, his Walk to Emmaus, and Pat wrote him the following letter:

> Dear Gus –
> I wish I could be there for your award—of all the "doers" in our family, you're the real star. I sometimes wish we could go back 50 years to our little act and change places—except I couldn't play the harmonica. Gus, God only knows what would

have happened to me if you hadn't been there—eight times I have had close calls—from cannon explosion—heart by-pass—arm burned badly—3 major internal operations and now my throat surgery and you and your prayers have always pulled me thru—I'd trade my career and fans for yours any day—we still have to drive thru Alabama and go back to the old town's mining camps and crossroads where Mother and Dad served the church and see our childhood together one more time.

I love you, and love to your family.

Pat

⇝   ⇜

In a *Times Daily* newspaper article, written by Entertainment Editor Terry Pace, Pat's niece Mary is quoted: "When Clinton and Gore first got elected and went into office, it really amused Uncle Pat. He couldn't believe how the Hollywood community was so taken with that whole country-boy image they tried to project. Uncle Pat would always say, 'I'm from Alabama—I can see right through that.'"

KMPC radio switched formats, so Chuck Southcott started another station, KJQI in Los Angeles, with the same format that KMPC used to have. On July 28, 1993, his show had a very notable guest. "Pat came in and spent an hour with me one day and was my guest host. We had a great time," he says. "This will give you the era: Leno had been doing *The Tonight Show* for a year or two, and Pat said, 'Seems to me Johnny's been taking a lot of vacation lately,' which is a typical Buttram line. It just comes out of left field and you can't help but laugh."

This was a show primarily about music and some recordings were played; however, Chuck and Pat talked about many topics during this hour—among them was voice work for Disney films and politicians, for which Pat had provided jokes. When Southcott brought up his guest's health, Buttram casually mentioned having had a polyp removed from his throat, but said that his overall health was just fine. He would rather have made their listeners happy with jokes and light banter than cause them concern by indicating how serious his throat condition had been and the suffering its treatment had caused him.

"He was an extremely funny man, but behind that curtain of funny-ness, which was well honed, was an extremely crafted writer and performer, and a very meaningful, sensitive man," said Maxine Hansen. "I think

I could've had a very meaningful conversation with this man about life. I think he had a lot to stay, but I don't think anybody tapped into it."

There was a story that Gene and Pat both loved to tell. "Gene would tell it, and Pat would tell it, then they'd flip coins to see who would tell it," laughs Chuck Southcott. "The story is that Gene was thinking about hiring Pat as his co-star, as his sidekick [many decades ago]. He arranged for them to meet at a restaurant in Hollywood known as the Brown Derby, a very famous place. Pat went into the restaurant and looked all around for Gene Autry. The time had come and he said he couldn't find him. He went into the bar, walked up to the bar and said to the bartender, 'I'm supposed to meet Gene Autry here. Have you seen him?' The bartender said, 'You're standing on him.' They got more mileage, both of them, from that joke for years. They'd tell it whenever they had important guests. Sometimes Gene would tell it, sometimes Pat would tell it, but it always got a laugh."

Gus and his wife Becky celebrated their fiftieth wedding anniversary in 1993. To help them celebrate, Pat had a fresh rose dipped in twenty-four-karat gold and sent it to them.

Back in Los Angeles, the Disney casting director asked Pat to provide the voice for the Possum Park Emcee in another of their animated productions, *A Goofy Movie*. This would be his final film. It was a musical, and the score represented the differing tastes of two generations, father and son, in a story about this unique relationship.

November was a big occasion for the family. Pat's aunt, Helen Maxwell Jenkins, was having her one-hundredth birthday. Pat wasn't able to be there in person, but he sent gifts for everyone. "He gave me a champagne bottle filled with jellybeans," says Hallie. He also had a friend drive the guests everywhere they wanted to go and gave them tickets to the museum. It was an exciting time for everyone.

Little did they know the next time they would see Pat, their laughter would be replaced with tears.

⋙   ⋘

Cancer had again plagued Pat. He developed a tumor that blocked the bile duct in his liver. Several therapies were tried. Nothing helped. Toxins built up in his organs and bloodstream, and the cancer spread. One by one, his organs shut down.

Early in the morning of Saturday, January 8, 1994, Pat drew his final breath at the UCLA Medical Center. He was seventy-eight.

Almost as if expressing the grief of the whole world, Los Angeles experienced a 6.7 earthquake shortly after Pat's death.

A private funeral was held on January 14 at Maxwell Chapel Methodist Church in the Pebble Community of Alabama. Officiating was Rev. Jonathan Todd, Rev. Bert Goodwin (husband of Pat's niece), and Rev. Bob Jenkins (Pat's cousin).

He was buried in the Maxwell Chapel cemetery, near Haleyville, by his parents' graves. Pat's tombstone is inscribed on both sides. On one side is the name he was given at birth. On the other side is written, under his stage name, "A man deserves paradise who can make his companions laugh."

⇥   ⇤

"Memorial services for Pat were held by the Pacific Pioneer Broadcasters at the Sportsman's Lodge in North Hollywood with more than 700 members attending," says Sue Clark Chadwick. "Tributes were given by many, including Gene Autry, Hal Kanter, Les Tremayne and Ralph Edwards. There was a real outpouring of love and respect."

Here is the first portion of Edwards' tribute:

> Well, who's going to make us laugh now, oh Lord? Who's going to slip into our Pacific Pioneer Broadcasters' meetings and ease up to us and before we can say "Howdy," Pat Buttram's laid out two or three rounds of high humor on us which might be called "country," but which is more accurately a "piece of art"; and that's only the precursor of two or three dozens or more true down-home, honest-to-goodness belly laughs of which the majority, or all, were of Pat's invention.

> Pat Buttram was and always will be a keepsake; an honest to goodness, down-home, one-liner, later nurtured, no doubt, in his rides into our town (Pat never called Hollywood a "city") en route to big doings for charity—or auditorium money-raiser for another needy health agency—or just to pat a fellow on the back; and when he really wanted to just be with his "people," a luncheon of the Pacific Pioneer Broadcasters, or a meeting with some cronies who always added Pat to their get-togethers because life sailed a lot lighter with Pat in the wings!

He answered every meaning of friendship.

Through the years Pat Buttram was our tonic—anytime—anywhere. You get sick, he'd have you on your feet in nothing flat—laughing! He visited me when I was in the hospital several years ago, and he had me out of bed in three minutes. The doctor came in to check me and asked Pat to leave—not because Pat was disturbing me—but because the doctor wanted Pat to go over and entertain the guys in sick bay!

⇥   ⇤

Pat's pal Gene Autry now had a huge void in his life. His buddy was gone. Autry's wife Jackie recalls, "When Pat passed away, Gene took it very hard and I could see tears in his eyes whenever anyone brought up his name. You see, they both had been through both good times and bad times together, and they were almost like brothers."

Referring to the *Readers' Digest* feature "My Most Unforgettable Character," Donna Martell says Pat would rank at the top of such a list. "He was a good man and he did a lot of good things."

"He was warm and—in this town it's rare—he was honest. He was genuine," agrees Randal Malone.

Robert Fuller misses Pat greatly. "The Golden Boot went downhill when they lost him as an emcee," he says. "Without Pat, it just wasn't the same. He was so sharp. He had the best barbs and best hooks that drove everybody to the wall…He was a very bright man. He's a legend. The man is a legend in this business."

Johnny Western adds, "His mind for comedy was very, very sharp. Categorically, that took him out of the realm of 'hick comedian.' He was much, much more than that."

⇥   ⇤

"The best piece of advice he ever gave me was given posthumously and I don't think he intended me to see it," says daughter Kerry. "In November 1993, Dad flew up here for Thanksgiving. Though he didn't feel well, he passed it off as a temporary illness. It wasn't until after he passed away (less than two months later) that we found, scrawled on his Reno Air ticket envelope, these words: 'Life isn't fair. Quit whining and get on with it.' It was a note to himself. He knew he was dying."

⊱   ⊰

Pat's memory lives on. Many of his movies and television shows are now available on DVD, so we can enjoy his work whenever we wish. Too, his sound-alike nephew, John Buttram, carries on the family tradition of gentle humor. John is often called on to serve as emcee of the various western-themed festival shows and, if you closed your eyes, you would swear that was Pat himself at the microphone. The world is indeed very blessed to have had Pat and now John, who keeps his uncle's memory alive and makes us laugh once again.

Chapter Fifteen

Seven months after his passing, Pat was given a heartfelt honor at the Golden Boot Awards ceremony. "That would be the Reagan Award—a gorgeous bronze figure made by actor/artist George Montgomery. I accepted that award for Dad at the August 1994 Boot," says Kerry. "Gene presented it. I remember neither Gene nor I could actually lift the thing—it's that heavy." The cover of the program that year featured a beautiful double-sketch by artist Ivan Jesse Curtis of Pat as his two most famous characters, Autry's sidekick and Mr. Haney.

Six years later, a man named Mr. Aderholt was allowed to give a tribute to Pat and brother Gus at the House of Representatives. Here is what he said:

July 11, 2000

Mr. Speaker, on June 19, 1915, a star and a humanitarian was born. Maxwell Emmett, better known as "Pat" Buttram of Addison, Alabama, in Winston County brought laughter and untold hours of sheer enjoyment to citizens across this great Nation. His film career spans 46 years from the early days as Gene Autry's sidekick to his parts as a voice in four of Disney's animated movies. Millions of television viewers will remember Pat for his role as the affable Mr. Haney in the television series "Green Acres" and "Petticoat Junction." Pat had a keen wit in the style of Will Rogers and was a much sought-after speaker.

Pat was brought up in a Methodist parsonage, son of a circuit-riding Methodist minister. He was the seventh child in a family of five boys and three girls. Pat never forgot the early lessons taught by this strong, God-fearing family. Concern for others was a staple in the Buttram household. As Pat's fame grew, he used his celebrity status to perform in benefits and shared his time and talents to help those less fortunate. He never forgot his roots or the place he called home. He donated not only money, but also his time to help build Camp Maxwell near his home in Alabama. This camp has played an important part in the lives of youth and the handicapped.

Pat died in Hollywood, California, on January 8, 1994, and was laid to rest in his family church at Maxwell Chapel in Winston County, Alabama.

While maybe not as well known, Pat's older brother, Gus Buttram, who lives in my hometown of Haleyville, was equally committed to serving others. Gus was born on June 21, 1913. While in high school, Gus suffered a paralysis that was brought on by tuberculosis. After surgery and rehabilitation, he graduated from Altoona High School in Etowah County, Alabama. Following graduation from Athens State in 1942 with a bachelor's degree in science and history, Gus married Rebecca, better known as Becky Buttram, Eppes of Goodwater, Alabama, on January 18, 1943. He followed his father into the ministry as a fourth generation Methodist minister. His first church appointment was at Remlap Methodist Church in Blount County, Alabama. Over the next three decades he would have many assignments in north Alabama.

Gus and Becky's desire to serve others is unquestioned. Turning down more lucrative career paths, Gus and Becky enriched the lives of those they serve. Retiring in 1978, Gus and Becky live at Pebble, near Haleyville, in Winston County, Alabama. They take great pride in their children, Mary Buttram Young, who is a dialysis nurse at Helen Keller Hospital in Sheffield, Alabama and Marvin McDaniel, better known as "Mac" Buttram, who is pastor of St. Andrews United Methodist Church in Cullman, Alabama, and is a fifth generation Methodist minister.

Mr. Speaker, it is my privilege today to recognize these two brothers, Gus and Pat Buttram, for their unselfish service to others.

Yes, Pat and his siblings, because of their loving, spiritual upbringing and their inner strength that resulted, had each enjoyed successful lives. Peggy did beautiful things with flowers and cards, but was also very active in children's work, having written children's columns in the national Cokesbury publication. Mamie was known for making adorable Raggedy Ann and Andy dolls. Each niece and nephew was her favorite; she lavished her abundant love on them all. Johnny was a very gifted businessman. Corry was loved by everyone who met him. Hallie's flower arrangements have won many awards. Gus is a beloved minister and the cofounder of Camp Maxwell. But it was their baby brother, Pat, who brought worldwide recognition to the Buttram name.

"He didn't limit himself," says WLS personality and historian Jeff Davis. "He had a background similar to mine and succeeded. He was a role model." George Lindsey felt the same way many years ago when he was breaking into the business.

"Pat was a comic genius," adds Bob Simons. "His facial expressions and timing were impeccable." Simons, a former disc jockey from Pennsylvania and Ohio, so enjoyed doing Pat Buttram impressions on the air, that folks still call him "Mr. Haney."

We will never know how many people have been influenced by this one man. True, Pat didn't command million-dollar contracts as a superstar would, but he had a brilliance, integrity, and generosity that were worth much more. He had the respect and love of his peers, and he was able to do for a living what he most enjoyed doing—making people laugh.

Appendix

Plays

1934   *The Heathers at Home* Birmingham-Southern College

Radio

As a Regular:

1934   WSGN, Birmingham, Alabama

1934-1948   WLS, Chicago, Illinois, Includes his own shows, Pat *Buttram's Radio School for Beginners, Jes' Startin'* and *Buttram's Palatial Palace of Wonders*

1948-1956   *Melody Ranch*, CBS

1957-1960   *Just Entertainment*, CBS, every weekday

1961-1965   *Story-Line,* KNX, Los Angeles, California, every day

1966   KGBS, Los Angeles, California

1989-1992   KMPC, Los Angeles, California

As a Guest:

1979   *Sears Radio Theater*, "Fontaine Harris, Le Baron de Parse," 4/10/79

1979   *Sears Radio Theater*, "Fontaine Harris in Hollywood," 7/24/79

1986   *The Dick Cavett Comedy Show*, 1/27/86

Motion Pictures

1943	*National Barn Dance* (Paramount Pictures)
1948	*The Strawberry Roan* (Gene Autry Productions)
1949	*Riders in the Sky* (Gene Autry Productions)
1950	*Mule Train* (Gene Autry Productions)
	Beyond the Purple Hills (Gene Autry Productions)
	Indian Territory (Gene Autry Productions)
	The Blazing Sun (Gene Autry Productions)
1951	*Gene Autry and the Mounties* (Gene Autry Productions)
	Texans Never Cry (Gene Autry Productions)
	Silver Canyon (Gene Autry Productions)
	Hills of Utah (Gene Autry Productions)
	Valley of Fire (Gene Autry Productions)
1952	*The Old West* (Gene Autry Productions)
	Night Stage to Galveston (Gene Autry Productions)
	Apache Country (Gene Autry Productions)
	Barbed Wire (Gene Autry Productions)
	Wagon Team (Gene Autry Productions)
	Blue Canadian Rockies (Gene Autry Productions)
1961	*Wild in the Country* (Twentieth Century-Fox)
1963	*Twilight of Honor* (MGM)
1964	*Roustabout* (Hal Wallis Productions/Paramount Pictures)
	The Hanged Man (Revue Studios/TV)
1965	*Sergeant DeadHead* (Alta Vista Productions/American International Pictures)
1968	*The Sweet Ride* (Twentieth Century-Fox/Euterpe Inc.)
	I Sailed to Tahiti with an All Girl Crew (National Telefilm Association/United National)
1970	*The Aristocats* (Walt Disney Pictures)
1972	*Evil Roy Slade* (Universal TV)

1973	*Robin Hood* (Walt Disney Pictures)
	The Gatling Gun (Broadway Enterprises/Universal Entertainment)
1976	*Joys* (Hope Enterprises)
1977	*The Rescuers* (Walt Disney Pictures)
1979	*The Sacketts* (MB Scott/Media Productions/Shalako)
	Angels' Brigade (Arista)
1981	*The Fox and the Hound* (Walt Disney Pictures)
	Choices (Oaktree)
1982	*Sonic, the Hedgehog*
1988	*Who Framed Roger Rabbit?* (Amblin/Silver Screen/Touchstone)
1990	*Return to Green Acres* (Arnold Productions/JayGee Productions/Orion TV)
	Back to the Future, Part III (Universal Pictures/Amblin Entertainment)
1995	*A Goofy Movie* (Walt Disney Pictures)

Television Series

1950-1956	*The Gene Autry Show* (sidekicks, Hap Wallace, Pat Jensen, Patrick Smith & Pat Buttram)
1958?	*The Pat Buttram Show* (himself)
1965-1971	*Green Acres* (Eustace Charleton Haney)
1979-1981	*The New Misadventures of Ichabod Crane* (voice)
1987—1989	*Melody Ranch Theater* (himself)
1990	*Gravedale High* (voice)
1991-1993	*Harvey Shine Presents*

Television Guest Appearances

| 1955 | *The George Gobel Show* (himself) |

1961	*Hot Off the Wire*, "Once Upon a Moose"
1962	*The Real McCoys*, "Luke the Reporter" (Pat Clemens)
	The Ed Sullivan Show, March 11, 1962 (himself)
1963	*The Ed Sullivan Show*, February 24, 1963 (himself)
	The Ed Sullivan Show, May 26, 1963 (himself)
	The Real McCoys, "The Partners" (Pat)
	The Ed Sullivan Show, August 4, 1963 (himself)
	Make Room for Daddy, "Here's the $50 Back"
1964	*The Ed Sullivan Show*, January 19, 1964 (himself)
	The Alfred Hitchcock Hour, "The Jar" (Charlie Hill)
	The Tycoon, "The Shotgun Meyer" (Brian)
	The Ed Sullivan Show, September 6, 1964 (himself)
	The Alfred Hitchcock Hour, "Lonely Place" (Emery)
1965	*The Munsters*, "All-Star Munster" (Pop Mallory)
	The Cara Williams Show, "Paradise Lost and Found" (Charlie Paradise)
	The Cara Williams Show, "Paradise Freezes Over" (Charlie Paradise)
	Vacation Playhouse, "Down Home" (Hardy Madison)
1966	*Petticoat Junction*, "The County Fair" (Mr. Eustace Charleton Haney)
	Pistols 'n' Petticoats, "A Crooked Line" (Pa Turner)
1967	*Pistols 'n' Petticoats*, "The Golden Fleece" (Jake Turner)
	The Ed Sullivan Show, March 26 (himself)
	The Hollywood Squares, May 15 (himself)
1968	*The Dean Martin Show*, March 14 (himself)
	The Wild, Wild West, "The Night of the Camera"
1969	*Petticoat Junction*, "The Other Woman" (Mr. Haney)
	Petticoat Junction, "A Most Momentous Occasion" (Mr. Haney)
1970	*Love, American Style*, "Love and the Longest Night"
	The Merv Griffin Show, June 25 (himself)

1971	*The Jimmy Stewart Show*, "Luther's Last Love" (Oscar Pettywhistle)
1972	*Alias Smith and Jones*, "Bad Night in Big Butte"
	Love, American Style, "Love and the Country Girl"
1973	*Adam-12*, "Keeping Tabs" (drunk man)
	The Dean Martin Show, "Celebrity Roast: Ed McMahon" (himself)
	The Dean Martin Show, "Celebrity Roast: Bette Davis" (himself)
	The Bobby Darin Show (himself)
1974	*Love, American Style*, "Love and the Competitors"
	Emergency!, "Floor Brigade" (Hermit)
	More Milton Berle's Mad World of Comedy special (himself)
1977	*Chico and the Man*, "Gregory Peck Is a Rooster" (Jed Gibson)
1978	*Just for Laughs* (himself)
1979	*The Dukes of Hazzard*, "Days of Shine and Roses" (Sam)
1980	*Uptown and Country* (himself)
1981	*Darkroom*, "The Partnership" (Tad Miller)
1982	*Simon & Simon*, "Rough Rider Rides Again" (Jonathan Evans)
	Father Murphy, "John Michael Murphy, R.I.P."
1983	*The Fall Guy*, "Happy Trails" (himself)
	The Love Boat, episode 6.27 (the chef)
	The Love Boat, episode 6.28 (the chef)
1984	*Family Feud*, "Country & Western Singers vs. TV & Film Cowboys"
1986	*Knight Rider*, "Fright Knight" (Buck)
1988	*Garfield and Friends*, "The Legend of Polecat Flats" (Voice of Cactus Jake)
	Garfield and Friends, "Cactus Jake Rides Again" (Voice of Cactus Jake)
	The Good, the Bad, and Huckleberry Hound (Voice of bartender Red Eye)

1989	*Garfield and Friends*, "Cactus Makes Perfect" (Voice of Cactus Jake)
1990	*Garfield and Friends*, "Urban Arbuckle" (Voice)
	Who's the Boss?, "Broadcast Blues" (Chappy)
1991	*Tiny Toon Adventures*, "Son of Wacko World of Sports" (Voice of Bicycle Bob)
	Who's the Boss?, "The Road to Washington," parts one & two (Chappy)
	Rugrats (Voice of Eddie)
1993	*Biography*, "Gene Autry" (himself)

Recordings

Singles:	*Get Up Early in the Morning/Mom's Golden Coffee Pot* (Filmways Records)
LPs (solo):	*We Wuz Poor* (Ovation)
	Laffter Sweet and Profane (KNX)
	Off His Rocker! (Warner Bros.)
LPs and CDs (with others):	*The Comedy Show/Spot with Dick Cavett* (Clayton Webster Corp.)
	Holidaytime with Gene Autry (Canadian)
	Jimmy Wakely Plus Movie Friends (Cattle Compact)
	The Funniest Roasts of the Century, Volumes one & two (Laugh.Com)

Newspaper/Magazine Columns

"Buttram Butts In"	*Stand By* (WLS-radio)
"Whittlin's"	*Stand By* (WLS-radio) and *Rural Radio*
"Pat Buttram Sez"	*Hollywood Citizen-News*, then nationally syndicated

Books *Poems for Out-Loud Readin': Gotten Together by Pat Buttram* (© 1960, Pat Buttram)

Baseball Joke Book (© 1972, Pat Buttram Co.)

Television Writing

1966   NBC special *Danny Thomas Goes Country and Western*

1972   CBS series, *The Jerry Reed When You're Hot You're Hot Hour*

????   Documentary, *The Movies That Saved a Generation*

Index

Breinigsville, PA USA
30 November 2010
250353BV00005B/14/P

9 781593 934262